HIGHER

COMPUTING
2008-2012

First exam published in 2008.
Published by Bright Red Publishing Ltd, 6 Stafford Street, Edinburgh EH3 7AU
tel: 0131 220 5804 fax: 0131 220 6710 info@brightredpublishing.co.uk www.brightredpublishing.co.uk

ISBN 978-1-84948-285-1

A CIP Catalogue record for this book is available from the British Library.

Bright Red Publishing is grateful to the copyright holders, as credited on the final page of the Question Section, for permission to use their material. Every effort has been made to trace the copyright holders and to obtain their permission for the use of copyright material. Bright Red Publishing will be happy to receive information allowing us to rectify any error or omission in future editions.

HIGHER

2008

[BLANK PAGE]

X206/301

NATIONAL
QUALIFICATIONS
2008

MONDAY, 2 JUNE
9.00 AM – 11.30 AM

COMPUTING
HIGHER

Attempt **all** questions in Section I.

Attempt **all** questions in Section II.

Attempt **one** sub-section of Section III.

Part A	Artificial Intelligence	Page 11	Questions 18 to 22
Part B	Computer Networking	Page 15	Questions 23 to 26
Part C	Multimedia Technology	Page 18	Questions 27 to 30

For the sub-section chosen, attempt **all** questions.

Read all questions carefully.

Do not write on the question paper.

Write as neatly as possible.

SECTION I

Attempt all questions in this section.

Marks

1. Images are stored as *bit-mapped* or *vector* graphics.

    (*a*)   (i)   Decribe how **bit-mapped** images are stored.   1

         (ii)   Describe how **vector** images are stored.   1

    (*b*)   Is the above image bit-mapped or vector? Justify your answer.   2

2. Anti-virus software uses various techniques to detect viruses. One of these techniques is *heuristic detection*.

    (*a*)   Explain how the heuristic detection technique is used to detect a virus.   1

    (*b*)   Explain why a *trojan horse* is **not** classified as a computer virus.   1

3. What is the decimal representation of the 8 bit *two's complement* number 10110110?

         A   −182

         B   −74

         C   −53

         D   182   1

4. (*a*)   The processor has a number of control lines. What is the function of the *reset* line?   1

    (*b*)   Explain why the *address bus* in a computer is unidirectional.   1

5. (*a*)   A *virus checker* and a *disk defragmenter* are *utility programs*. Name **one** other utility program.   1

    (*b*)   Explain how the use of a **disk defragmenter** can improve the system performance of a computer.   2

Marks

SECTION I (continued)

6. Two network topologies are shown below.

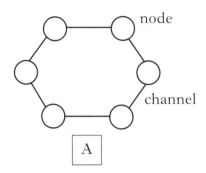

(*a*) (i) Identify the network topology of Network A.   1

     (ii) Identify the network topology of Network B.   1

(*b*) Which of the above topologies would be **least** affected by a channel failure?   1

7. Numbers can be stored within a program as *integer* or *real* variables.

Explain what is meant by an "integer" variable.   1

8. One task of the evaluation stage of the software development process is to ensure the program meets the *software specification*.

(*a*) State **two** other criteria used to evaluate software.   2

(*b*) Describe what is meant by the phrase "the software development process is an iterative process".   1

9. A bank manager uses a *macro* once a month to create an alphabetical list of customers whose account balance is over £5000.

(*a*) State **two** benefits of using macros for this type of task.   2

(*b*) The macro is written in a high level language. State the **type** of high level language that is used to write macros.   1

10. A program contains the following statement:

is_a (rover, dog).

State which **type** of programming language is being used.   1

[Turn over

Marks

SECTION I (continued)

11. A holiday booking website includes a currency converter which asks for the amount in pounds sterling and converts it to euros. Here is the top-level algorithm, including data flow for steps 1 and 2.

    1.   get amount of pounds   (out: **pounds**)

    2.   calculate euros   (in: **pounds** out: **euros**)

    3.   display conversion   ....

    (*a*) State which *design notation* is being used.   **1**

    (*b*) Step 3 results in the following being displayed on screen:

                  £500 converts to 750 euros.

        State the *data flow* for step 3.   **2**

    (*c*) Identify whether the **pounds** variable in step 1 should be passed *by value* or passed *by reference*. Explain your answer.   **2**

12. Explain the purpose of a CASE statement in a high level language.   **2**

                                      (30)

[END OF SECTION I]

Marks

SECTION II

Attempt all questions in this section.

13. When designing a new computer the manufacturer could improve system performance by increasing the *clock speed* or adding more *RAM*.

   (*a*) (i) Describe one **other** way to improve the system performance **and** explain why it would be effective.   2

        (ii) Explain why it is **not** possible to keep improving performance by increasing clock speed.   1

   (*b*) (i) Describe how *FLOPS* **and** *application based tests* are used to measure system performance.   2

        (ii) Explain why application based tests could be described as the best measure of system performance.   1

        (iii) Explain why FLOPS could be described as the best measure of system performance.   1

   (*c*) A new computer system has a 3 GHz processor with a 64-bit data bus and a 32-bit address bus. Calculate the maximum amount of memory that can be addressed by this computer. Show all working and express your answer in appropriate units.   3

   (*d*) Describe how a processor distinguishes one memory location from another.   1

[Turn over

Marks

SECTION II (continued)

14. The proposed layout of a new office network is shown below. Cables are used to connect the network.

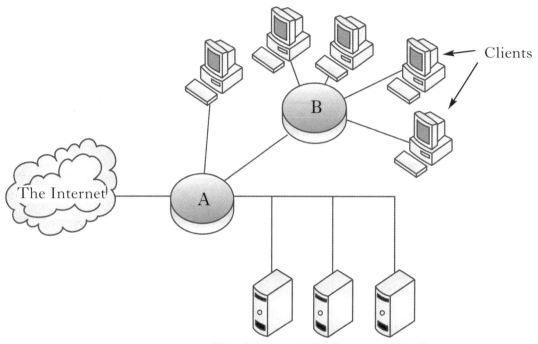

(a) A router and a hub are used in the above network.

   (i) State which device, A or B, is the router. State **one** reason to justify your choice of device.   **2**

   (ii) State which device, A or B, is the hub. State **one** reason to justify your choice of device.   **2**

(b) After the network has been installed, it is discovered that data traffic on the network is slow.

   (i) State **one** technical change which could be made to improve network performance.   **1**

   (ii) Explain how this change will improve network performance.   **1**

(c) Name a **type** of server that allows Web pages to be accessed within a LAN.   **1**

Marks

SECTION II (continued)

15. James wants to make copies of some photographs. He intends to use a scanner to capture the photographs and an ink jet printer to print the final images.

    (*a*) State the function of the operating system that is responsible for the data transfer between the processor and scanner.   1

    (*b*)   (i) Explain why saving the scanned image as a *gif* would **not** be appropriate in this case.   1

        (ii) State a suitable file format for saving the file.   1

    (*c*) The scanner is set to a resolution of 1200 dpi using *24 bit colour depth* and the photographs are 6 inches by 8 inches. Calculate the uncompressed size of the file. Express your answer in appropriate units. Show all working.   3

    (*d*) One function of the printer interface is to inform the processor that it is ready to receive the next photograph. State the name of this function.   1

    (*e*) State **one** advantage of using *serial* over *parallel* transmission when sending data to a printer.   1

    (*f*) State **one** technical characteristic that the printer should have. Justify your answer.   2

    (*g*) When James prints his images he discovers lines across some of them. The lines are where the original photographs had been folded over.

        Explain why he would use a bit-mapped package to remove the lines.   2

[Turn over

Marks

SECTION II (continued)

16. An international athletics competition between eight countries has a number of events. Here are the results for one race.

Lane Number	Country	Time (secs)
1	Ireland	40·23
2	Italy	41·05
3	England	42·88
4	France	39·89
5	Germany	40·55
6	Poland	40·01
7	Scotland	39·87
8	Wales	42·55

The stadium's computer system has a program which processes and displays the results.

(a) State **two** system requirements that would have been specified for the installation of the program.   2

(b) The program is modular. State **two** benefits of creating modular code.   2

(c) At the end of a race, messages are displayed. For example:

> **Winner: Sco 39·87**

The winning country for a race is stored in a string variable called **winner**.

Using code from a programming environment with which you are familiar, show how to extract the first three characters from the variable **winner**.   2

(d) The program stores the list of race times in a single data structure.

(i) State the data structure and data type used to store the race times.   2

(ii) The program must find the fastest time for a race. Use pseudocode to design an algorithm to find the fastest time.   4

(iii) It is suggested that it would be preferable for the algorithm to find the **lane number** of the fastest time rather than the fastest time. Explain how this could be achieved.   1

Marks

SECTION II (continued)

17. Entucom is a television broadcaster that gives customers access to various services. Customers will access these services using their television and a set-top box with wireless keyboard and mouse.

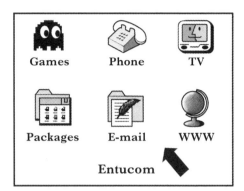

The television broadcaster employs a software development company to provide the range of software required.

(a) The software development company appoints a *systems analyst* during the analysis stage of the software development process.

　　(i) Describe **two** tasks carried out by the systems analyst.　　2

　　(ii) State **two** benefits that the analysis stage has for the **remaining** stages of the software development process.　　2

(b) During implementation, the software development company consider the use of either a *procedural* or an *event-driven* language.

　　(i) Describe **two** similarities of **procedural** and **event-driven** languages.　　2

　　(ii) State **two** reasons why a programmer would use an **event-driven** language to develop software.　　2

(c) During the development of the software, *module libraries* are used. The modules limit the *scope* of certain variables.

　　(i) What is a **module library**?　　1

　　(ii) Describe **one** way in which the **scope** of a variable may be limited.　　1

　　(iii) Explain why the programmer might want to **limit** the scope of a variable.　　2

(d) The software developed should be subject to testing using a comprehensive set of **test data**. State **two** other methods of testing comprehensively.　　2

(e) Entucom insist that the software is *portable*. Explain why portability is important in this situation.　　1

(f) New set-top boxes may be developed in the future. State which type of maintenance could be required to ensure the software works with the new boxes. Explain your answer.　　2

(60)

[END OF SECTION II]

SECTION III

Attempt ONE sub-section of Section III

For the sub-section chosen, attempt *all* questions.

SECTION III   *Marks*

Part A—Artificial Intelligence

Attempt all questions.

18. Archaeologists are still exploring areas of the Great Pyramids in Egypt. These pyramids have a maze of tunnels with sharp turns and sudden drops. Unknown routes through tunnels are explored by robots such as Pyramid Rover. The robot is operated by humans from a control room.

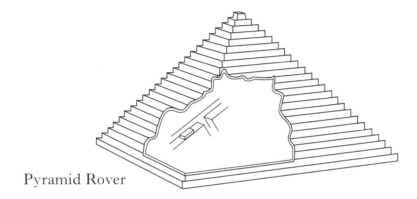

Pyramid Rover

   (*a*) State **two** reasons why Pyramid Rover has its movement controlled by humans.   2

   (*b*) Describe **two** practical problems that had to be overcome when the Pyramid Rover was designed.   2

   (*c*) Despite having its movement controlled, Pyramid Rover is classed as an *intelligent robot*, rather than a *dumb robot*.

   (i) Describe **one** situation where Pyramid Rover would **need** intelligence as well as, or instead of, user control.   1

   (ii) Explain how Pyramid Rover would apply intelligence in this situation.   1

   (*d*) After using the control software on Pyramid Rover, the archaeologists ask for several new features to be added. Name this type of software maintenance.   1

19. Computer games have been available since the 1960s.

   (*a*) State **two** differences that a **user** of modern computer games would notice compared to these early games.   2

   (*b*) State **two** benefits that modern software development environments offer programmers of current games.   2

   (*c*) (i) Explain how the use of parallel processors has aided the performance of computer games.   2

   (ii) Other than parallel processing, state **two** other advances in hardware which have led to improvements in the performance of computer games.   2

   (iii) Explain how each of these advances has led to this improvement in performance.   2

Marks

SECTION III

Part A—Artificial Intelligence (continued)

20. (*a*) Artificial Intelligence programming languages are categorised as either *functional* or *declarative* (logic).

    (i) Name a functional language.   **1**

    (ii) Name a declarative language.   **1**

    (iii) State whether the following section of code is written using a functional or a declarative language.   **1**

```
(defun eliza ()
    "Respond to user input using pattern matching rules."
    (loop
        (print 'eliza>)
        (write (flatten (use-eliza-rules (read))) :pretty t)))
```

(*b*) *Semantic nets* are used to represent knowledge before coding.

Use a semantic net to represent the following information about some herbs.

Mint and basil are herbs.
Pennyroyal and spearmint are types of mint.
Genovese basil and purple basil are two types of basil.
Mints can be used in making tea, basil is used in the making of pesto.

6

Marks

SECTION III

Part A—Artificial Intelligence (continued)

21. SHRDLU is a program which uses *natural language processing* (NLP) to manipulate blocks of various colours, shapes and sizes. An initial setup of the objects is shown below.

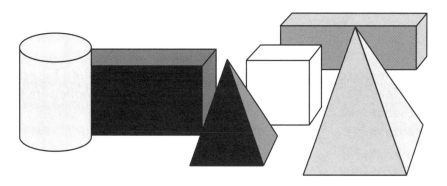

SHRDLU understands commands such as:

```
put the grey cylinder on top of the black block
put the white cube in front of the grey block
```

(*a*) Here are two commands from a SHRDLU dialogue. What is the problem with each command?

    (i)   `put it on its side`

    (ii) `put the pyramid on the grey block`   1

(*b*) SHRDLU will accept the command   1

    `grasp the grey block`

Explain why SHRDLU might not understand the following command:

    `grip the grey block`

(*c*) State **one** reason why there are more problems with natural language processing than with more formal programming languages.   1

(*d*) In speech recognition software, there are four main stages of NLP. The first is speech recognition and the last is speech synthesis. Name the remaining **two** stages.   1

(*e*) Eliza is an application of NLP. Explain how Eliza responds to user input.   2

      2

[Turn over

Marks

SECTION III

Part A—Artificial Intelligence (continued)

22. There have been nine manned Apollo space flights to the moon. Six have landed astronauts on the surface of the moon. Two of the crew would land on the moon whilst the other would remain in orbit.

   The following is an extract from a knowledge base recording space expeditions to the moon.

```
1   apollo(7, schirra, eisele, cunningham).
2   apollo(8, borman, lovell, anders).
3   apollo(11, armstrong, collins, aldrin).
4   apollo(12, conrad, gordon, bean).
5   apollo(13, lovell, swigert, haise).
6   apollo(16, young, mattingly, duke).
7   apollo(17, cernan, evans, schmitt).

8   crew_landed_on_moon(A) IF apollo(A,_,_,_) AND
                              A>10 AND
                              not(A=13).



9   walked_on_moon(X,Z) IF  apollo(A, X,_,Z) AND
                            crew_landed_on_moon (A).
```

On Apollo 7, Schirra, Eisele and Cunningham were the crew.

A landed on the moon if A was an Apollo mission and the flight was after Apollo 10 and A was not 13.

Astronauts X and Z walked on the moon if X and Z were the first and third crew members of Apollo A and Apollo A landed on the moon.

Note: *The underscore '_' in lines 8 and 9 is used when the value of the argument is irrelevant to the rule and can be ignored.*

   (a) Use the line numbers to identify an example of each of the following in the above program:

   (i) a fact;   **1**

   (ii) a rule.   **1**

   (b) Name the **two** search techniques used in artificial intelligence.   **2**

   (c) State the solution to the query:

   `?apollo(A, armstrong, Y, aldrin).`   **2**

   (d) Trace the first solution to the query:

   `?walked_on_moon(conrad, bean).`

   In your answer, you will be given credit for the correct use of the terms "sub-goal" and "instantiated".   **8**

   (e) Explain why there is a problem with the solution to the following query:

   `?walked_on_moon(duke, young).`   **2**

(50)

[END OF SECTION III—PART A]

Marks

SECTION III

Part B—Computer Networking

Attempt all questions.

23. Ditton High School plans to set up a network of computers throughout the school. The school is made up of three separate buildings. Within each building a wired network is created. Wireless technology is used to share data between the buildings.

    (a) Describe **one** economic reason why the school would have chosen to connect the school buildings using wireless technology.   1

    (b) Describe **two** reasons in favour of using a *star* topology rather than a *bus* topology in each of the separate buildings.   2

    (c) The school network consists of 256 devices. Which *class* of IP address should be used within the network?   1

    (d) Describe **one** implication of a network being allocated an inapproriate class of IP address.   1

    Two methods used by the school to protect the network and the pupils are a *firewall* and a *walled garden*.

    (e) Describe how a **firewall** protects a local area network with an Internet connection from outside attacks.   1

    (f) Why would the school have decided to set up a **walled garden**?   2

24. Mel is creating a website to show images and video clips from a recent holiday. The homepage contains the title "Mel's Website". The title is in bold and italics.

    (a) Write the *HTML* code required for the title.   3

    (b) Mel publishes her webpage and submits the page to various *meta-search engines*. Describe how a **meta-search engine** operates.   2

    (c) Describe in detail how the increase in the availability of ADSL connections has affected the design of web pages.   2

    (d) The TCP/IP protocol will be used when uploading certain files. Describe **two** operations carried out by the TCP part of the protocol.   2

    (e) State which layer of the *OSI model* is described by the following:

       (i) "provides a means for the user to access information on a network using appropriate software";   1

       (ii) "translates data into a format suitable for the other layers to deal with".   1

    (f) The OSI model describes seven layers or levels. State **one** benefit of breaking the process of network communication into different layers.   1

Marks

SECTION III

Part B—Computer Networking (continued)

25. Module libraries are to be used in the development of a piece of software that will be used to transfer data across a local area network.

    (a) State **two** reasons why the use of module libraries speeds up the development of software. 　　2

    (b) The program can allow data to be sent *synchronously* or *asynchronously*.

    Describe asynchronous data transmission. 　　2

    (c) Data can be sent using *packet switching* or *circuit switching*.

    Describe fully **one** advantage of packet switching over circuit switching. 　　3

    (d) Error checking is an essential component of data transmission. *Parity check* is one method of error checking.

    　　(i) Describe **one** instance where a parity check would not detect an error that has occurred during transmission. You should use an example to illustrate your answer. 　　2

    　　(ii) Name **one** other method of **detecting** data transfer errors within a network. 　　1

    　　(iii) Describe how this method works. 　　2

    (e) "Error checking increases data transfer time whilst improving network performance."

    Justify this statement. 　　2

Marks

SECTION III

Part B—Computer Networking (continued)

26. Gordon frequently accesses websites as part of his work as a salesman.

(a) Gordon enters the URL of a site he wishes to visit. This URL is sent to a *domain name server* to be resolved.

What occurs during domain name resolution?   2

(b) Describe **two** reasons why a domain name server may be unable to resolve a URL.   2

(c) Gordon lives in a rural village where high speed Internet access is not available through telephone or cable lines. However, he often works at home using his laptop to connect to the company server.

   (i) State **one** way in which Gordon could obtain high speed Internet access.   1

  (ii) Describe **two** security issues that Gordon's employers will have to consider when allowing their employees to remotely access the company server.   2

 (iii) Other than allocating usernames and passwords, describe how each of the security issues you have described in part (ii) could be overcome.   2

(d) Gordon creates a *wireless personal area network* (WPAN).

   (i) Other than a desktop or laptop computer, state **two** other devices commonly found in a WPAN.   2

  (ii) Describe **two** reasons why Gordon would create a WPAN with these devices.   2

Gordon's managers are concerned over possible misuse of the IT equipment issued to their staff. They begin to check the content of their employees' e-mails.

(e) (i) State the Law which allows the managers to carry out these checks.   1

  (ii) Describe **two** other surveillance activities that this Law allows employers or the police to carry out.   2

                                      (50)

[END OF SECTION III—PART B]

Marks

SECTION III

Part C—Multimedia Technology

Attempt all questions.

27. A multimedia application called "Chef" is to be created to accompany a new cookbook. The software development process is applied to the creation of "Chef" software.

   (a) The purpose of the multimedia application is one aspect which must be investigated during the *analysis* stage.

      State **two** other aspects which must also be investigated.   2

   (b) Presentation software allows the inclusion of media elements and the use of hyperlinks to move between pages.

      Describe **two** advanced features of authoring software which make it more suitable for creating a multimedia application.   2

   (c) Describe **two** ways in which "Chef" should be tested.   2

   (d) When "Chef" is released, it is distributed along with software used to view the application.

      (i) State **two** benefits of this distribution method for the user.   2

      (ii) State **one** benefit of this distribution method for the software development team.   1

   The performance of a multimedia application can depend on the hardware components of the system. These could include a powerful processor and the use of *holographic storage*.

   (e) Explain how the use of a more powerful processor will benefit the performance of a multimedia application.   2

   (f) Explain how **holographic storage** can be used to store terabytes of data.   2

   (g) Other than processing and storage, name **one** development in computer **hardware** and describe how it has supported advances in multimedia.   2

Marks

SECTION III

Part C—Multimedia Technology (continued)

28. The image shown below is being used in the advertising campaign for a new dog biscuit called "Bonzo Bites".

(*a*) The original image is a bitmap file.

Explain the purpose of a *CLUT* in this file format.   1

(*b*) Describe a benefit of using a CLUT when applying effects to a bitmap image.   1

The biscuit name was created using graphics software. It was saved as a graphic file type. It is shown below.

Bonzo Bites

(*c*) (i) State the technique that could be applied to the text to improve its appearance.   1

(ii) Explain how the use of this technique improves the appearance of the text.   2

The text is added onto the image. The text appears in a white box as shown below.

(*d*) (i) Name the feature which will avoid showing the white box.   1

(ii) Name **one** graphics file format that provides this feature.   1

Marks

SECTION III

Part C—Multimedia Technology (continued)

28. (continued)

(e) The image file is edited and saved as a compressed bitmap file.

   (i) Describe how the *RLE* compression method reduces the file size.   2

   (ii) Explain why this compression method may **not** be effective on this image file.   2

(f) *Object oriented* data storage is more efficient than *bitmap* storage.

   (i) Explain when this statement is **not** true.   2

   (ii) Name and describe **one** file type suitable for 3D object oriented data storage.   2

29. A website is being developed for Write Rhymes, a company that writes poems and rhymes.

(a) A video clip is placed on the home page. It contains a child introducing the company by reciting a rhyme. The video will be played using *streaming*.

   (i) What is meant by the term "streaming"?   1

   (ii) Describe **one** reason why it was decided to stream the video clip.   1

(b) The video clip was recorded using 15 frames per second in 24 bit colour depth with 600×800 pixels. The clip lasts for 2 minutes.

Calculate the file size of the video clip. Ignore sound and compression in your calculation. Show all working and express your answer in appropriate units.   3

(c) The font used on each page was specially created for Write Rhymes. When the pages are viewed by potential customers they see a substitute font instead.

What should have been done to ensure this font is shown correctly?   1

(d) On the birthday rhyme page, audio clips of sample rhymes can be played. Each rhyme is stored as a *RIFF* file.

   (i) Name the *codec* used by RIFF.   1

   (ii) Describe the technique used for compression by this *codec*.   1

(e) The rhymes are recorded in mono.

Explain why the recording was not made in stereo.   1

(f) Copyright is held by Write Rhymes for all content on the website.

Describe **two** examples of how users could breach copyright.   2

Marks

SECTION III

Part C—Multimedia Technology (continued)

30. A choir use a recording studio to produce their own CD.

(a) The vocals for each track are captured using *digitised sound*.

Explain the term "digitised sound".   **1**

(b) The backing music for each track is an instrumental MIDI file.

(i) State **one** reason why MIDI would produce a high quality sound.   **1**

(ii) MIDI has a small file size compared to digitised sound.

State **one** further benefit that MIDI has over digitised sound.   **1**

(iii) State **two** reasons why some musical artists do not use MIDI.   **2**

(c) The vocals and backing music are combined to produce each completed track.

Name **two** features of sound editing software and explain how **each** may be used to improve the completed track.   **4**

(50)

[END OF SECTION III—PART C]

[END OF QUESTION PAPER]

[BLANK PAGE]

HIGHER
2009

[BLANK PAGE]

X206/301

NATIONAL
QUALIFICATIONS
2009

THURSDAY, 4 JUNE
9.00 AM – 11.30 AM

COMPUTING
HIGHER

Attempt **all** questions in Section I.

Attempt **all** questions in Section II.

Attempt **one** sub-section of Section III.

For the sub-section chosen, attempt **all** questions.

Read all questions carefully.

Do not write on the question paper.

Write as neatly as possible.

SECTION I

Marks

Attempt all questions in this section.

1. (a) Write the binary number 1000100111 as a **positive** integer.   1

   (b) Represent the decimal number −73 using 8 bit *two's complement*.   1

2. Most modern computers use *Unicode* rather than *ASCII* to represent text.

   State one **advantage** of Unicode when compared to ASCII.   1

3. State the number of bits required to represent 16 777 216 colours.   1

4. System software consists of the operating system and utility programs.

   (a) A *disk editor* is a common example of utility software. Describe **one** function of a disk editor.   1

   (b) The *bootstrap loader* is part of the operating system. State the purpose of the bootstrap loader.   1

5. A *trojan horse* is a malicious computer program. State **one** characteristic of a trojan horse.   1

6. Explain why increasing the number of *registers* could improve system performance.   1

7. A piece of software has been installed on a computer. A compatibility issue may prevent the new software from running properly on the computer.

   (a) State **one** possible **software** compatibility issue that might prevent the new software from running.   1

   (b) State **one** possible **hardware** compatibility issue that might prevent the new software from running.   1

8. A company is advised to change from a *peer-to-peer* network to a *client-server* network.

   (a) Describe **one** difference between a peer-to-peer network and a client-server network.   2

   (b) Describe **one** possible technical reason for choosing a client-server network over a peer-to-peer network.   1

Marks

SECTION I (continued)

9. A graphic file is to be transferred as an e-mail attachment. Explain why a *JPEG* file might be preferred to a *TIFF* file for the graphic in this situation.

    2

10. The software development process is described as an *iterative* process.

    Explain how the iterative nature of the software development process is used in the production of software.

    2

11. The *software specification* can act as part of the legal contract between the client and the software development company.

    State **two** other purposes of this document.

    2

12. A program is being designed which generates a username using the following steps:

    1.   get user initial and surname
    2.   create username
    3.   display the username

    (*a*) Show how these steps could be represented using a *graphical design notation*.

    2

    (*b*) The username is created by joining the initial to the end of the surname, for example "CarrickE".

    Name the *string operation* used to create the username.

    1

13. Many applications contain scripting languages.

    Explain why there is a need for scripting languages within applications.

    1

14. Name **one** type of personnel involved in the *documentation* stage.

    1

15. Software can be evaluated in terms of *robustness* and *reliability*.

    (*a*) Explain what is meant by the term "robustness".

    1

    (*b*) Explain what is meant by the term "reliability".

    1

[Turn over

Marks

SECTION I (continued)

16. Software may require adaptive maintenance when a new operating system is installed.

    Describe **one** further example of when adaptive maintenance would be required.   **1**

17. A program is created during the implementation stage of the software development process.

    (*a*) Programmers may make use of a *module library*. State what is meant by the term "module library".   **1**

    (*b*) The program may require a *user-defined function*. State what is meant by the term "user-defined function".   **2**

    (30)

[END OF SECTION I]

Marks

SECTION II

Attempt all questions in this section.

18. A palmtop computer has a processor with a 24 bit address bus, 32 bit data bus and 8 control lines. The palmtop computer accepts *flash cards* as additional storage.

   (a) The processor receives a signal on an *interrupt* control line. Explain what happens when the processor receives the signal.   2

   (b) Calculate the **maximum** amount of memory that the palmtop computer can address.

   Express your answer in appropriate units. Show all working.   3

   (c) Data is to be transferred from the processor to main memory using a *write* operation.

   Describe how a processor would perform a **write** operation. Your answer should mention the *buses* or *control lines* used at **each** stage.   4

   (d) A file created on the palmtop is to be stored on the flash card. The *file management* and *input/output management* functions of the palmtop's operating system are used during the transfer.

   Describe **one** task carried out by **each** of these functions.   2

   (e) The price of *flash cards* has decreased in recent years as their capacity has increased.

   State **one** other recent trend in the development of flash cards.   1

19. Pat has a *wireless enabled* laptop in his house. He uses this to **illegally** access his neighbour's wireless network.

   (a) Name the Act of Parliament that makes this network access illegal.   1

   (b) Pat's computer has anti-virus software installed. One technique used by anti-virus software to **detect** a virus is *virus signature recognition*.

      (i) Name **one** other virus **detection** technique.   1

      (ii) Describe how the technique you named in part (i) detects a virus.   1

      (iii) Describe how a virus might use *camouflage* to **avoid** virus signature recognition.   1

[Turn over

Marks

SECTION II (continued)

20. A network is configured as a *star* topology. It contains **four** computers and a *switch*.

    (*a*) Draw a **labelled** diagram of this star topology. You should **clearly** show the location of the **switch**.   2

    (*b*) Describe **one** advantage of using a *star* topology compared to a *bus* topology.   1

    (*c*) Explain why using a *switch* rather than a *hub* may improve the performance of a network.   2

    (*d*) Explain why the addition of a print server to a large network contributes to an improvement in network performance.   1

    (*e*) Developments in *browser software* have contributed to the increase in the use of networks.

    Describe **two** of these developments.   2

21. One function of an *interface* is to store data in transit between the computer and a peripheral.

    (*a*) State **one** other function of an interface.   1

    (*b*)   (i) Describe how data is transferred using a *serial interface*. You may include a diagram in your answer.   2

         (ii) Describe how data is transferred using a *parallel interface*. You may include a diagram in your answer.   2

    (*c*) State **one** advantage of a serial interface over a parallel interface.   1

Marks

SECTION II (continued)

22. NoTow is a company running a city centre car park. The company requires software to control the operation of the car park. The software will have modules for actions such as "recognising a car is at a barrier", "printing an entry ticket" and "calculating ticket charge".

(a) Name the most suitable **type** of programming language to implement this software. Explain your answer.

2

(b) The software is written using modules. Describe **two** benefits to the programmer of writing modular code.

2

(c) After the software is written, testing is carried out.

   (i) "Testing should be planned in advance with the creation of a test plan containing the test data to be used and the expected results."

   State the **aspect** of testing being described here.

1

   (ii) "Testing should be as thorough and complete as possible covering every part of the program with all kinds of test data and testers."

   State the **aspect** of testing being described here.

1

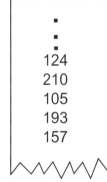

NoTow would like the software to calculate the number of cars on a particular day that spent more than three hours in the car park. The number of whole minutes each car is parked in the car park is stored in a list, as shown on the right.

(d) Use *pseudocode* to design an algorithm to carry out this calculation.

4

(e) The output from part (d) is turned into a percentage of the total number of cars using the car park in a day. This is stored in a variable called **percent**.

Using a programming language with which you are familiar, show how to format the output to **two** decimal places.

2

(f) Identify the **type** of *maintenance* used to add the module described in part (d). Justify your answer.

2

[Turn over

Marks

SECTION II (continued)

23. A cinema ticket system allows customers to select and pay for their own tickets.

    The top level algorithm is:

    1. Get ticket details
    2. Calculate cost
    3. Display cost and accept payment

    The module **CalculateCost** uses the number of tickets and the category of ticket to calculate the total payment due. It uses the *parameters* described below.

Parameter	Description
Amount	Number of tickets
Category	Adult, child, student, OAP
Cost	Total cost of required tickets

    (a) State the most suitable *data type* for the parameter called **Cost**.   1

    (b) Parameters can either be passed by *value* or by *reference*.

       (i) Identify **one** parameter that is passed **by value** to the module **CalculateCost**. Justify your answer.   2

       (ii) Identify **one** parameter that is passed **by reference** to the module **CalculateCost**. Justify your answer.   2

    (c) A program may use *local* variables and *global* variables.

       (i) What is the *scope* of a **global** variable?   1

       (ii) State **two** advantages of using *parameter passing* rather than *global* variables when programming.   2

    (d) State **one** reason why *portability* of software is an important factor for developers to consider.   1

Marks

SECTION II (continued)

23. (continued)

(*e*) To calculate the total cost, the program must check the category of each ticket against the four possible categories. The programmer could use **a series of IF statements** or a **nested IF** as shown below.

Series of IF statements:

IF category = 'adult' THEN Price=5.50

IF category = 'child' THEN Price=3.50

IF category = 'student' THEN Price=4.50

IF category = 'OAP' THEN Price=4.00

Nested IF:

If category = 'adult' THEN
    Price=5.50
ELSE IF category = 'child' THEN
    Price=3.50
ELSE IF category = 'student' THEN
    Price=4.50
ELSE IF category = 'OAP' THEN
    Price=4.00
END IF

(i) The programmer decides to use a nested IF. Explain why this is a more **efficient** method.   2

(ii) State **one** other *multiple outcome selection* statement that the programmer could have used.   1

(*f*) The program will make use of a *1-D array*.

(i) When creating, or declaring, a 1-D array for use in a program, a name must be given to the array.

State **two** other items that should be specified when the array is created.   2

(ii) Explain why it is a more *efficient* use of system resources to pass an array **by reference** rather than **by value**.   2

(60)

[END OF SECTION II]

[Turn over

SECTION III

Attempt ONE sub-section of Section III

For the sub-section chosen, attempt *all* questions.

SECTION III

Marks

Part A—Artificial Intelligence

Attempt all questions.

24. A human tester communicates with one human and one computer using remote terminals. The tester is to identify which terminal is connected to the human and which is connected to the computer.

   (*a*) State the name of this test.   1

   (*b*) State **one** limitation of this test.   1

   (*c*)   (i) State **one** strategy that the human tester could use to differentiate between the human and the computer.   1

       (ii) Explain why the strategy suggested in (*c*)(i) helps the tester to tell the difference between the human and the computer.   1

25. *Natural Language Processing* (NLP) involves creating software that uses language in a similar way to people.

   (*a*) State **two** common applications of NLP.   2

   (*b*) NLP has to deal with *ambiguity of meaning* in sentences.

       (i) Describe what is meant by "ambiguity of meaning" in a sentence.   1

       (ii) The speech recognition stage of NLP correctly recognised the following sentences.

         Sentence 1   "The man threw a bottle at the window and broke it."

         Sentence 2   "The restaurant was full of international food specialists."

         State **one** example of ambiguity from **each** sentence.   2

   (*c*) Name the stage of NLP that would attempt to resolve ambiguity in a sentence.   1

   (*d*)   (i) Name the stage that takes place after your answer to (*c*).   1

       (ii) Explain why it is important to deal with ambiguity prior to this stage.   1

   (*e*) Regional accents or pronunciations, as well as ambiguity, can cause problems for NLP.

       State **two** other problems for NLP, using an example to illustrate each answer.   4

[Turn over

Marks

SECTION III

Part A—Artificial Intelligence (continued)

26. A bicycle manufacturer is developing an *expert system* to advise customers on their bicycle purchase.

    (a) State **one** reason why the bicycle manufacturer's *domain* is suitable.   **1**

    (b) The following paragraph contains some of the information for the proposed expert system.

    > Racing and mountain are two types of bicycle. Racing bicycles have drop handle bars. Hardtails and full-suspension are two types of mountain bicycle.

    Draw a *semantic net* to represent this information.   **4**

    (c) An expert system can be created using an *expert system shell*.

       (i) Name and describe **one** component of an expert system shell.   **2**

       (ii) State the component that must be added to an expert system shell to create an expert system.   **1**

    (d) Other than faster development time, state **one** advantage of creating an expert system using an expert system shell rather than a declarative language.   **1**

Marks

SECTION III

Part A—Artificial Intelligence (continued)

27. A *search tree* is shown below.

Node **L** is the **start**, or initial, state.

Node **N** is the **goal** state.

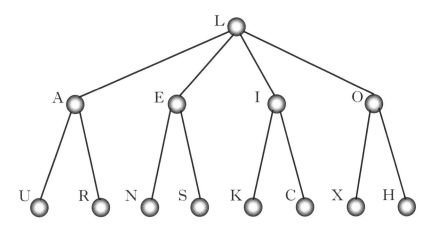

(a) State the order in which nodes would be visited using a *breadth-first* search, stopping when the goal state is reached. **1**

(b) (i) State the order in which nodes would be visited using a *depth-first* search, stopping when the goal state is reached. **1**

  (ii) List the nodes stored in *working memory* when the goal state is found using a **depth-first** search. **1**

  (iii) Explain your answer to (b)(ii) making reference to the search tree. **2**

(c) Search trees can result in *combinatorial explosion*.

  (i) Describe what is meant by a "combinatorial explosion". **2**

  (ii) The game of chess is one example of a problem that results in combinatorial explosion. State another example. **1**

  (iii) Describe how a heuristic search can be used to overcome the problems of combinatorial explosion. **2**

  (iv) Explain **one** way in which faster processors can improve the speed of a heuristic search. **1**

(d) Explain why the use of *cache memory* could improve search times. **2**

[Turn over

Marks

SECTION III

Part A—Artificial Intelligence (continued)

28. The following knowledge base contains information about various animals.

```
1  subclass(monotreme, mammal).        A monotreme is a subclass of mammal.
2  subclass(platypus, monotreme).
3  subclass(anteater, mammal).

4  has(bird, egg_laying).              Birds lay eggs.
5  has(mammal, live_young).            Mammals have live young.
6  has(mammal, warm_blood).

7  has(platypus, egg_laying).

8  has(X,Y) IF subclass(X,Z) AND has(Z,Y).  X has the property Y if X is a subclass of Z AND
                                            Z has the property Y.
```

(a) (i) State the answers to the query:

    `?-has(X, egg_laying).`   2

(ii) State the query for the question "What are the subclasses of mammal?".   1

(b) Assuming that a depth-first search is used, trace the first **two** solutions to the query:

    `?-has(platypus, Y).`

You must include the correct use of the term *sub-goal* in your trace.

Use the line numbers to help your explanation.   7

(c) Explain the difficulty with the answers to part (b).   1

(d) State the name of the type of rule used in line 8.   1

    (50)

[END OF SECTION III–PART A]

SECTION III
Part B—Computer Networking
Attempt all questions.

Marks

29. The diagram below shows the configuration of two *intranets*. Each LAN is connected to the Internet via a *router*.

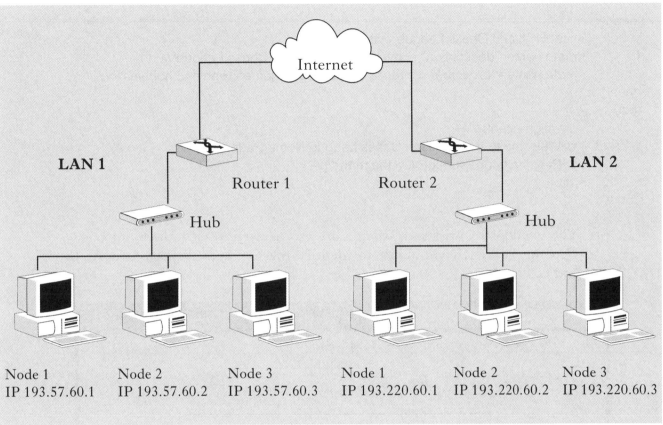

(a) (i) State the *class* of network for LAN 1. Justify your answer.   **2**

    (ii) State how many **additional** nodes can be connected to LAN 1. Justify your answer.   **2**

(b) Node 1 on each of the LANs has the same hardware specification and operating system.

    (i) State a possible reason why node 1 on LAN 2 may have a better performance.   **1**

    (ii) Justify your answer to part (i).   **1**

(c) State why it is possible for the three stations on LAN 1 to communicate if they have different operating systems.   **1**

A mail message is sent from node 1 on LAN 1 to node 3 on LAN 2 using *TCP/IP*.

(d) State a suitable *application layer* protocol when sending the message.   **1**

(e) Describe in detail the role of TCP when sending and receiving the message.   **3**

(f) A *Cyclic Redundancy Check* (CRC) is used to check the data packets for errors. Describe the operation of CRC.   **3**

(g) Describe how a router ensures that the data packets reach the **correct** destination.   **2**

Marks

SECTION III

Part B—Computer Networking (continued)

30. Hamish is creating a website for the Highland Chess League. Part of the *HTML* for the home page is shown below.

```
<head>
        <title>Highland Chess League</title>
        <meta name="description" content="The Highland Chess League"/>
        <meta name="keywords" content="chess,league,games,Highland,hobbies"/>
</head>
<body>
        <div align="centre">
        <p>Welcome to the Highland Chess League Home Page</p>
        <p>Play the board <u>not</u> the man</p>
        </div>
</body>
```

(a) The window below is seen when a browser is used to view the home page. Use the HTML code above to identify the contents displayed in A, B and C.

3

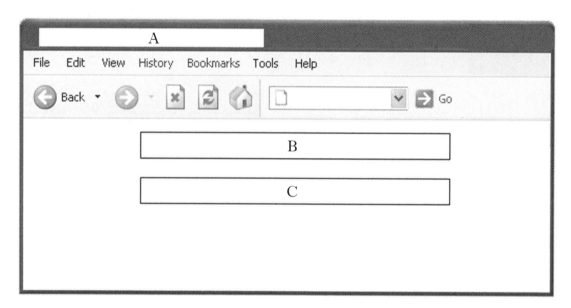

(b) Hamish uses *FTP* once he has developed the website. State what FTP is used for in this situation.

1

(c) (i) State the purpose of the following line of the HTML code.

2

```
<meta name="keywords" content="chess,league,games,Highland,hobbies"/>
```

(ii) Describe how a *spider* would use this line of code.

2

(iii) Explain why one search engine may provide more relevant and comprehensive results than another.

2

Marks

SECTION III

Part B—Computer Networking (continued)

30. **(continued)**

(*d*) Morag knows that Hamish is working on the website. She enters http://www.highlandchess.com into her browser and receives the following message.

The requested URL could not be retrieved

While trying to retrieve the URL:http://www.highlandchess.com

The following error was encountered:

DNS Server unable to resolve

    (i) Describe the events that led to this message being displayed.   **3**

    (ii) State what Hamish must do to make the website accessible to the public.   **1**

31. The owner of a local coffee shop has decided to provide Internet access for his customers. A computing company sends one of their personnel to examine the coffee shop and interview both the owner and the staff.

(*a*) State the **job title** of the person sent from the computing company.   **1**

(*b*) The coffee shop can either be wired with network access points in the wall or a wireless access point can be installed.

    (i) State **two** reasons why the wireless access point solution was chosen.   **2**

    (ii) State a suitable type of Internet connection for the coffee shop.   **1**

(*c*) The wireless network is correctly installed, but customers complain that at certain times the Internet access is very slow. State **one** reason for this drop in performance.   **1**

[Turn over

Marks

SECTION III

Part B—Computer Networking (continued)

32. A college intranet is used by lecturers, technicians and students. The technicians need to be able to install software and configure computers on the network.

(*a*) Explain how it is possible to allow **only** the technicians to install software.   1

(*b*) A hacker intercepts student records which are being sent between two lecturers.

    (i)   State the term used to describe this type of attack.   1

    (ii) Describe **one** software technique to defend against this type of attack.   1

(*c*) Explain the difference between a *backup strategy* and *disaster avoidance techniques*.   2

(*d*) A **differential** backup contains all files that have changed **since** the last **full** backup.

    (i)   State **one** advantage of using this type of backup compared to a full backup of data.   1

    (ii) Describe a situation where a differential backup would not provide any advantage over a full backup.   1

(*e*) The intranet is connected to the Internet. This may cause both **access** and **security** issues.

    (i)   Describe the technique known as *Internet filtering*.   1

    (ii) Describe the technique known as a *walled garden*.   1

(*f*) State **two** reasons why Internet filtering would be more appropriate for the college.   2

(*g*) *Application filtering* is a technique used by a firewall. Name and describe **one** other technique.   2

(*h*) Describe the meaning of the terms:

    (i)   data integrity;   1

    (ii) data security.   1

                                              (50)

[END OF SECTION III–PART B]

Marks

SECTION III

Part C—Multimedia Technology

Attempt all questions.

33. The company VideoStream specialises in video recording devices.

(a) Ten years ago, VideoStream's best selling product was their VS32 video capture card. Due to advances in video camera technology, the VS32 video capture card is no longer for sale.

   (i) One of the main components of the video capture card is the DSP. Describe the role of the DSP.   **1**

   (ii) Describe the technological advance in video cameras that has resulted in the drop in sales of **all** video capture cards.   **1**

(b) Derek has bought VideoStream's latest video camera that comes with free video editing software.

   (i) Derek records a two minute video using 24-bit colour and a 1000 by 800 pixel frame size at 10 frames per second. Calculate the file size of the uncompressed video. Show all working and express your answer in appropriate units.   **3**

   (ii) The settings in part (i) produced a poor quality video. Explain why the video is poor quality.   **1**

Derek records several video clips and tries out the free video editing software. He loads the video clips and then uses two features of the video editing software to edit the video as shown below.

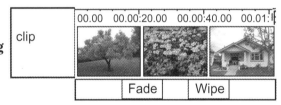

   (iii) Name **two** features of the video editing software that Derek has used to edit the video.   **2**

(c) The default format for saving video clips from all VideoStream's products is AVI. AVI is an example of a *container file*.

Explain why AVI is a "container file".   **1**

(d) MPEG is a compressed video file type. Describe how MPEG achieves compression.   **3**

[Turn over

Marks

SECTION III

Part C—Multimedia Technology (continued)

34. Harpreet is an experienced website creator. She uses a WYSIWYG editor rather than a text editor to create a website.

   (*a*) Compare the use of a WYSIWYG editor and a text editor in producing the website, in terms of their demand on system resources.   **2**

   (*b*) As part of a graphic for the website, Harpreet scanned the image of an eye using 24-bit colour.

      Describe how a scanner captures an image. Your answer must contain an appropriate level of technical detail.   **3**

   (*c*) After scanning, Harpreet scaled the eye and used *image manipulation software* to adjust the image.

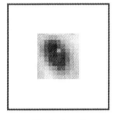  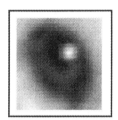

      Original   After   After
      scan   scaling   adjustment

     (i) Name the feature of image manipulation software that Harpreet used to carry out the adjustment.   **1**

     (ii) Explain how this feature is able to improve the image of the eye.   **1**

     (iii) Name and describe a *compression technique* that would allow Harpreet to reduce the file size of the 24-bit colour eye without losing any image quality when it is decompressed.   **2**

   (*d*) Harpreet would like music to be playing in the background while each web page is being viewed. The music can either be stored as a MIDI file or a compressed MP3 file.

     (i) Describe **one** way that the file size is reduced when saving a sound file as a compressed MP3 file.   **1**

     (ii) State **two** advantages of storing the music for Harpreet's web page using MIDI rather than MP3.   **2**

Marks

SECTION III

Part C—Multimedia Technology (continued)

35. The logo for a transport system was created as an *SVG* graphic and is shown on the right

(*a*) SVG is an example of a *vector graphic* file type. Name **one** other vector graphic file type.

1

(*b*) Explain why the above logo can be stored more **efficiently** as an SVG graphic than in the equivalent bit-map graphic.

1

(*c*) Choose **one** of the objects in the metro logo above and show how it would be represented in SVG code.

Your answer should include the **name** of the object and at least **two** attributes.

2

(*d*) A small part of the SVG code for the logo is shown below.

rgb(0,0,255)

   (i) State which colour is represented by this code.

1

   (ii) The largest number that can be entered in to the **rgb** instruction shown above is 255.

   Calculate the bit depth of that object. Show **all** working.

2

(*e*) The logo was converted to *3D* and a *texture* applied to it.

Explain the term "texture" in relation to 3D graphics.

1

(*f*) The logo was converted to a bit-map so it could be **animated.**

Name a bit-map format that would be suitable for storing the animated logo.

1

[Turn over

Marks

SECTION III

Part C—Multimedia Technology (continued)

36. FoneSmart is releasing the latest version of their highly successful smart phone.

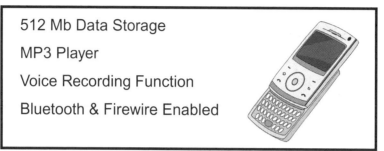

512 Mb Data Storage

MP3 Player

Voice Recording Function

Bluetooth & Firewire Enabled

(*a*) A multimedia presentation has to be designed and created for the launch of the latest version of the phone.

   (i) State **two** elements that should be included in the **design** of a multimedia presentation.   2

   (ii) Describe **two** reasons why FoneSmart may wish to create the presentation in *multimedia authoring* software rather than *presentation* software.   2

(*b*) The phone has a voice recording function. This allows the phone to record the user's voice using 8-bit mono sound at 22 kilohertz. The recording is then stored on a flash memory card.

   (i) Calculate the file size of a 30 second voice recording. Express your answer in appropriate units. Show all working.   3

   (ii) Calculate how many of these 30 second voice recordings can be stored on a 512Mb flash card. Show all working.   1

   (iii) One of the advantages of using a flash card in the phone, rather than optical or magnetic storage, is its portability.

   Describe **one** other advantage of using a flash memory card in the phone compared to optical or magnetic storage.   1

(*c*) Voice recordings may be stored using either *PCM* or *ADPCM*.

   (i) State **one** advantage of storing the recording using ADPCM compared to PCM.   1

   (ii) Describe how ADPCM stores sound data.   1

Marks

SECTION III

Part C—Multimedia Technology (continued)

36. (continued)

(d) FoneSmart have received complaints that some voice recordings are unclear. The waveform of one of these recordings is shown on the right.

Explain why this recording is unclear. 1

(e) Music files can be transferred to the phone by connecting the phone directly to a computer using either *Bluetooth* or *Firewire*.

(i) State **one** advantage of using "Bluetooth" rather than "Firewire" for transferring music files to the phone. 1

(ii) State **one** disadvantage of using "Bluetooth" rather than "Firewire" for transferring music files to the phone. 1

(f) Explain how this smart phone demonstrates *convergence of technology*. 1

(g) FoneSmart are designing a new smart phone that will use *holographic storage*.

This phone will have a larger storage capacity and a faster data transfer rate than previous phones.

(i) Explain how holographic storage achieves a very high storage capacity. 1

(ii) Explain how holographic storage achieves a very high data transfer rate. 1

(50)

[END OF SECTION III–PART C]

[END OF QUESTION PAPER]

[BLANK PAGE]

[BLANK PAGE]

X206/301

NATIONAL
QUALIFICATIONS
2010

THURSDAY, 3 JUNE
9.00 AM – 11.30 AM

COMPUTING
HIGHER

Attempt **all** questions in Section I.

Attempt **all** questions in Section II.

Attempt **one** sub-section of Section III.

Part A	Artificial Intelligence	Page 10	Questions 18 to 22
Part B	Computer Networking	Page 16	Questions 23 to 26
Part C	Multimedia Technology	Page 20	Questions 27 to 31

For the sub-section chosen, attempt **all** questions.

Read all questions carefully.

Do not write on the question paper.

Write as neatly as possible.

Marks

SECTION I

Attempt all questions in this section.

1. Convert this *8-bit two's complement* binary number into a decimal.

   11010011

   1

2. Jane is concerned about a virus infecting her computer.

   (a) *Watching* is one *virus code action*. Describe the term "watching".

   2

   (b) State **one** other virus code action.

   1

3. A *register* can be used to store a *memory address*. State the **two** other types of item that can be stored in a register.

   2

4. A new printer has 640 megabytes of RAM installed. State **one** reason why the printer has RAM installed.

   1

5. Complete the **two** missing stages of the *fetch-execute cycle*.

1	The memory address of the next instruction is placed on the address bus.
2	
3	The instruction is transferred to the processor on the data bus.
4	

   2

6. Greg buys a single copy of a popular computer game. He then makes several copies to give out to his friends.

   (a) State the name of the law that he has broken.

   1

   (b) State **one** reason why making copies of the game is illegal.

   1

7. Explain **one** difference between a *Local Area Network (LAN)* and a *Wide Area Network (WAN)* in terms of *transmission media*.

   2

8. Describe **one** reason for connecting a network using a *switch* rather than a *hub*.

   2

Marks

SECTION I (continued)

9. Most high level languages have several *data types* available.

   (*a*) State what is meant by a *real* variable.   **1**

   (*b*) State the most suitable *data structure* and *data type* for storing the list called "valid" in the pseudocode shown below.

   ```
   For each member of list
     If gender(current) = "M" or gender(current) = "F" Then
       Set valid(current) to true
     Else
       Set valid(current) to false
     End If
   End fixed loop
   ```
   2

10. *Design* is the second stage of the software development process.

   (*a*) Explain the importance of the design stage for one of the later stages in the software development process. Your answer should refer to the name of the stage that you have chosen.   **2**

   (*b*) Describe how *stepwise refinement* can be used to help produce a detailed design.   **2**

11. Documentation is produced at **each** stage of the software development process.

   (*a*) Name **one** item of documentation that is produced at the *implementation stage*.   **1**

   (*b*) One purpose of creating documentation at **each** stage is to provide a starting point for the next stage.

   State **one** other purpose of documentation.   **1**

   (*c*) Describe the role that the programmer might play in the production of the *technical guide* during the *documentation* stage.   **1**

12. Software can be evaluated in terms of *efficiency* and *portability*.

   (*a*) Software can be described as efficient if it does not waste memory.

   Describe **one** way of making software efficient in terms of **memory usage**.   **2**

   (*b*) Describe what is meant by the term "portability".   **2**

Marks

SECTION I (continued)

13. A sports centre has purchased software to assist with daily tasks such as bookings. The new software includes a *scripting language*.

    State **one** use of a scripting language. **1**

    (30)

[END OF SECTION I]

Marks

SECTION II

Attempt all questions in this section.

14. Carolyn uses a computer to edit photographs that she has taken with her digital camera.

    (a) When Carolyn switches on her computer, system software in ROM finds and loads the operating system. Name this system software in ROM.   1

    (b) Carolyn transfers the photographs from her camera to her computer using a *serial interface*.

        (i) Two functions of the interface are *data format conversion* and *handling of status signals*. Describe how each of these functions would be involved in this data transfer.   2

        (ii) State **two** other functions of an interface.   2

    Carolyn reduces the *bit-depth* of the photographs from 24 bits to 16 bits before saving the photographs onto the hard disk of her computer system.

    (c) (i) Describe **one** advantage of reducing the bit-depth of the photographs from 24 to 16.   2

        (ii) Describe **one** disadvantage of reducing the bit-depth of the photographs from 24 to 16.   2

        (iii) A 4 inch by 6 inch photograph with a resolution of 600 dpi and using 16-bit colour depth is stored. Calculate the file size of the photograph.

        State your answer using appropriate units. Show all your working.   3

    (d) Two functions of the operating system are *memory management* and *input/output management*. Describe the roles of each of these **two** functions when a photograph is saved on to the hard drive.   2

    (e) Carolyn's camera uses *solid state storage*. Explain **one** reason why solid state storage is used in digital cameras.   2

    (f) Carolyn uses photo editing software that allows her to store a photograph using *JPEG* or *GIF* file format. Describe **one** difference between these two file formats.   2

[Turn over

Marks

SECTION II (continued)

15. Ernie has bought a new computer with 24 *control lines*, a 32-bit *address bus* and a 64-bit *data bus*.

    (*a*) Calculate the **maximum possible** amount of memory that Ernie's computer can address. State your answer using appropriate units. Show all your working.   **3**

    (*b*) Ernie's computer has 16 megabytes of *cache* memory. Describe how the use of cache memory may improve system performance.   **2**

    (*c*) Ernie requires new word processing software to use on his computer system. Describe **one** *compatibility issue* that should be considered when buying new software.   **2**

    (*d*) Two methods of measuring performance are *application based tests* and *MIPS*.

        (i) Explain why MIPS may be the better measure of **processor** performance than application based tests.   **2**

        (ii) State **one** other measure of processor performance.   **1**

    Ernie's computer is part of a small *peer-to-peer network* of computers in his family home. There are three other computers in the house.

    (*e*) Explain **one** reason why the family created a *peer-to-peer* network instead of a *client-server* network.   **2**

Marks

SECTION II (continued)

16. Mrs Laird sets her Higher Computing class the task of writing a program that will take in three items – day, month and year. These three variables will have the same data type. The program will then output a "DateofBirth" variable with six characters, as shown below.

Input Variables		
day	month	year
15	Jun	1992

Output Variable
DateofBirth
150692

(a) State the only *data type* that the pupils can use for **all three** of the "day", "month" and "year" variables. Justify your answer. **2**

(b) Name the operation used to extract the last two characters from the contents of the "year" variable. **1**

(c) Part of the program will take the contents of **month** e.g. "Jun" and turn this into the corresponding **two** character value for that month e.g. "06". Mrs Laird tells the pupils they must **not** use IF statements to implement this part of the program.

Use pseudocode to design an algorithm for this part of the program. You should show only the first two months in your algorithm. **3**

(d) Name the operation used to join the three values together to produce the six characters for "DateofBirth". **1**

(e) The contents of the "DateofBirth" variable are to be held in memory in ASCII format. Calculate the mininum amount of memory required to store the contents of this variable. **2**

(f) The pupils are using a *procedural* language to write their programs.

   (i) State **two** features of procedural languages. **2**

   (ii) State **one** feature of *event-driven* languages that is **not** commonly found in procedural languages. **1**

(g) Mrs Laird tells the pupils that their programs must be easily *maintainable*. Describe **two** characteristics of a program that make it easily "maintainable". **2**

(h) Mrs Laird also tells the pupils that they must avoid the use of *global variables* in their programs where possible.

   (i) State the meaning of the term "global variable". **1**

   (ii) Explain why the pupils have been asked to avoid the unnecessary use of global variables when programming. **2**

[Turn over

Marks

SECTION II (continued)

17. Henry works for a company that maintains office buildings. He decides to write a program to print labels for the room keys in a new office block. The block has 38 floors, each with 25 rooms. The label will consist of the floor number and the room number. The design for the program is shown below alongside a sample section of output.

```
For each of 38 floors
    For each of 25 rooms
        Display "Floor Number:" and floor_no
        Display "Room Number:" and room_no
    Next room
    Display two blank lines
Next floor
```

Floor Number: 12
Room Number: 3
Floor Number: 12
Room Number: 4

(a) Once the program has been written it must be translated. Describe clearly why using a *compiler* to translate the code produced from **this** algorithm would be more efficient in terms of **processor usage** than using an *interpreter* to translate the same code.   2

(b) State **one** example of how text output from a program could be *formatted*.   1

(c) The company decide to include Henry's code as a new function in their building management software.

State the **type** of maintenance being carried out on the building management software by adding this section of code as a subprogram.   1

(d) In order for Henry's program to operate correctly for **any** office building **two** parameters would have to be passed to it.

   (i) State what these **two** parameters would be.   2

   (ii) State whether these parameters would be passed to the subprogram by *value* or by *reference*. Justify your answer.   2

(e) Another subprogram in the building management software is used to find the range of temperatures in a building in one day. The temperature is recorded every 15 minutes within a 24 hour period and stored in a list.

Use pseudocode to design **one** algorithm to find **both** the **highest** and **lowest** temperatures in this list.   5

(60)

[*END OF SECTION II*]

SECTION III

Attempt ONE sub-section of Section III

For the sub-section chosen, attempt *all* questions.

Marks

SECTION III

PART A—Artificial Intelligence

Attempt all questions.

18. Game playing is one area of research in *artificial intelligence*. Computers are being used in games such as chess and card games.

   (a) (i) State **one** meaning of the term "artificial intelligence".   1

       (ii) Name **one** popular test used to determine whether a computer system can be described as having artificial intelligence or not.   1

      (iii) Explain why training computer systems to play simple games is thought to be a good way of investigating artificial intelligence.   2

   (b) (i) One aspect of intelligence is *cognitive ability*. State **two** other aspects of intelligence that are used in game playing.   2

       (ii) Describe how **each** of your answers in part (i) may be used in game playing.   2

   (c) *Parallel processing* and *increased memory* have improved the performance of computers in game playing.

        (i) Describe how parallel processing can improve performance in games such as chess.   2

       (ii) Describe how increased memory can improve performance in games such as chess.   2

Marks

SECTION III

PART A—Artificial Intelligence (continued)

19. An area of artificial intelligence attempts to model systems based on the human brain. A diagram of a neuron found in the human brain is shown below.

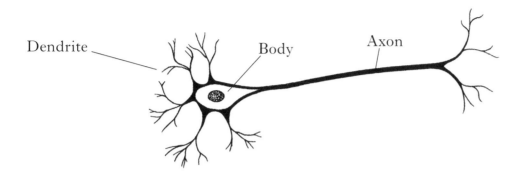

   (a) Describe **one** similarity between an *artificial neuron* and a human neuron.   **1**

   (b) State **two** changes that can take place within an *artificial neural system* during the learning (or training) process.   **2**

   (c) In order to develop an artificial neural system a *restricted domain* should be identified.

      (i) Explain what is meant by the term "restricted domain".   **1**

      (ii) State **one** other characteristic of a domain suitable for implementing as an artificial neural system.   **1**

   (d) The artificial neural system can be *hard-wired* or implemented as a *software model*.

      State **one** advantage of implementing an artificial neural system as a software model instead of being hard-wired.   **2**

20. A company has developed a computer vision system to monitor swimmer safety in outdoor swimming pools. The system monitors activity in the pool using a number of cameras and will alert lifeguards to potential problems.

   (a) *Computer vision* consists of a number of stages.

      (i) Name and describe the **first** stage of computer vision.   **2**

      (ii) *Edge detection* will be used to analyse the image. Explain **one** problem for edge detection in **this** situation.   **2**

   (b) The cameras capture still images using **65536** colours. Calculate the *bit depth* of the images captured.   **1**

Marks

SECTION III

PART A—Artificial Intelligence (continued)

21. A student has created software about extinct animals for a museum. The software has a *knowledge base* with information about animals and the century in which they became extinct.

```
1    extinct(dodo seventeenth)
2    extinct(sea_cow eighteenth)
3    extinct(atlas_bear nineteenth)
4    extinct(rice_rat twentieth)
5    extinct(eastern_elk nineteenth)
```
The dodo became extinct in the seventeenth century.

```
6    older(seventeenth eighteenth)
7    older(eighteenth nineteenth)
8    older(nineteenth twentieth)
```
The seventeenth century is older than the eighteenth century.

```
9    earlier(A B) IF older(A B)
```
Century A is earlier than century B if century A is older than century B.

```
10   earlier(A B) IF older(A C) AND
                    earlier(C B)
```
Century A is earlier than century B if century A is older than century C and century C is earlier than century B.

```
11   extinct_earlier(X Y) IF extinct (X A) AND
                            extinct (Y B) AND
                            earlier (A B)
```
Animal X became extinct earlier than animal Y if animal X became extinct in century A and animal Y became extinct in century B and century A is an earlier century than B.

(a) State the solutions to the following query:

```
? extinct(X nineteenth)
```
2

(b) When testing the knowledge base the student entered a query to identify the centuries that came before the twentieth century.

The solutions to the query were:

```
A = nineteenth
A = eighteenth
A = seventeenth
```

State the query that the student entered that resulted in this output.

3

Marks

SECTION III

PART A—Artificial Intelligence (continued)

21. (continued)

(c) Trace the **first** solution to the query:

```
? extinct_earlier(X sea_cow)
```

In your answer you will be given credit for the correct use of the term *sub-goal*.   **6**

(d) *Negation* is implemented in Prolog by the use of *NOT*. Describe the effect of *NOT* in the evaluation of a query.   **1**

(e) The knowledge base could have been represented using a *semantic net*.

(i) Draw a simple semantic net of the fact at line 7.   **2**

(ii) Use your diagram to explain how a semantic net is used to represent knowledge.   **2**

(f) The student chose to implement the software using a *declarative* language rather than a *procedural* language.

One reason for this choice was the facility to use *facts* and *rules*. State **one** other reason for choosing a declarative language.   **1**

[Turn over

Marks

SECTION III

PART A—Artificial Intelligence (continued)

22. A *search tree* is shown below. The *goal state* is represented by the node C.

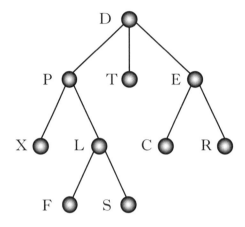

Depth-first and *breadth-first* are search techniques that may be used to find the goal state.

(*a*) State the order in which nodes would be visited using **depth-first**, stopping when the goal state is reached.   1

(*b*) (i) State **one** advantage of using **depth-first** when compared to breadth-first to search the tree.   1

   (ii) State **one** advantage of using **breadth-first** when compared to depth-first to search the tree.   1

(*c*) (i) State which one of these two search techniques makes use of *backtracking*.   1

   (ii) Explain how the search technique named in part (*c*) (i) employs backtracking when searching the tree shown above.   2

(*d*) The most *efficient* search would visit the nodes in the order **DEC**. This would use a *heuristic search*.

   Describe how a heuristic search finds the nodes in the path **DEC**.   3

   (50)

[END OF SECTION III—PART A]

[Turn over for Question 23 on *Page sixteen*

Marks

SECTION III

PART B—Computer Networking

Attempt all questions.

23. The manager of the Sea Bay Hotel has created a website to display details of the hotel and allow customers to make online bookings.

She hopes that this will cut down on the number of errors in bookings, such as double-booking and employees entering the wrong details for bookings.

(*a*) The web address for the Sea Bay Hotel is:

www.seabayhotel.co.uk

A user enters this web address into a browser. Describe how the *domain name server* uses the web address to access the website.   **3**

(*b*) Online hotel booking systems may be subject to additional problems such as hacking and credit card fraud.

Name and describe **one** other possible illegal activity that the hotel could suffer from as a result of allowing customers to book and pay online.   **2**

(*c*) The hotel uses an intranet with ten computers, two printers and a scanner connected to it.

State the most suitable class of *IP address* for this network. Justify your answer.   **2**

(*d*) The manager is concerned about employees accessing unsuitable websites from the hotel's computers.

   (i) Describe how *Internet filtering software* would prevent employees from accessing unsuitable websites.   **1**

   (ii) Describe how a *walled garden* would prevent employees from accessing unsuitable websites.   **2**

(*e*) Despite these precautions, the manager suspects that an employee is accessing websites containing illegal material.

State **two software** actions that the *Regulation of Investigatory Powers Act* would allow the police to undertake.   **2**

(*f*) The Sea Bay Hotel website can be found by using a *search engine*. A search engine can use either a *spider* or a *meta-search*.

Describe how **each** of these two methods is used by a search engine.   **2**

Marks

SECTION III

PART B—Computer Networking (continued)

23. **(continued)**

    (*g*) Some of the *HTML* coding for the hotel website is shown below.

    ```
    <html>
    <head>
    <title><i>Sea Bay Hotel Home Page</i></title>
    <body>
    <center><h1>Sea Bay Hotel</h1></center>
    <p>Welcome to the Sea Bay Hotel</p>
    </body>
    </htm>
    ```

    Identify **two** errors that are present in the above HTML code.   2

    (*h*) Describe **two** changes that could be made to the HTML code of the webpage to increase the number of hits by a search engine, once the above errors have been corrected.   2

    (*i*) The manager is worried about *viruses*. *Anti-virus software* has been installed on all of the hotel computers.

    Name and describe **one** class of virus that the anti-virus software might detect.   2

24. Legends is a catering company that owns 130 restaurants nationwide. Each restaurant is connected to the head office through a Wide Area Network (WAN) to allow communication and file sharing.

    (*a*) The network uses *CSMA/CD*.

        (i) Describe how CSMA/CD operates.   4

        (ii) State **one** way in which CSMA/CD **reduces** network performance.   1

    (*b*) The TCP/IP protocol uses *packet switching* when transmitting files over the network. Explain **one** advantage of packet switching over *circuit switching* when transmitting files over a network.   2

[Turn over

Marks

SECTION III

PART B—Computer Networking (continued)

25. Bishopsland High School has its computers connected in a Local Area Network (LAN). The network is connected using cables.

    (a) The network conforms to the *Open Systems Interconnection* (OSI) model.

    Two layers of the OSI model are the *Session layer* and the *Network layer*.

    (i) State **one** task carried out at the Session layer. 1

    (ii) Name a networking device that operates at the Network layer. 1

    (b) Data can be sent over a network using *synchronous* or *asynchronous* data transmission.

    Explain **one** advantage of synchronous compared with asynchronous data transmission. 2

    (c) A 200 megabyte file is to be downloaded at 100 megabits per second.

    Calculate how many seconds it will take to download the file. Show all working. 2

    A pupil has suggested that a wireless network would be better than the current cable network.

    (d) (i) Name a **hardware** device that must be present in a computer to enable it to connect to a wireless network. 1

    (ii) Explain the function of this device. 1

    (e) State **two** disadvantages of converting to a wireless network compared to using cables. 2

    (f) The school network has been subject to a *denial of service* attack.

    Describe **one** method of using software to carry out a denial of service attack. 1

    (g) The school is situated in a remote area that was previously considered *Information Poor*.

    (i) Describe **one** way that the pupils may now be *Information Rich*. 1

    (ii) Explain **one** social implication of the change to Information Rich. 1

Marks

SECTION III

PART B—Computer Networking (continued)

26. When data is transmitted across a network, it is important that error checking takes place.

   A *parity check* and a *cyclic redundancy check* are two methods of error checking.

   (*a*) Explain why a cyclic redundancy check is more effective than a parity check.   2

   (*b*) *Error checking* improves the **integrity** of data passing through the network.

   Explain **one** way that error checking may **reduce** the performance of the network.   2

   (*c*) The network must be able to avoid catastrophic failure. Describe **two** software *disaster avoidance* techniques that could be used to make the network less prone to failure.   2

   (*d*) If the disaster **avoidance** techniques fail, the network may crash. A *backup server* and *mirror disks* are both *backup strategies* that could be used to **recover** from this disaster.

   (i) Describe **one** benefit and **one** drawback of using a backup server as a disaster recovery strategy.   2

   (ii) Describe **one** benefit and **one** drawback of using a mirror disk as a disaster recovery strategy.   2

   (50)

[END OF SECTION III—PART B]

Marks

SECTION III

PART C—Multimedia Technology

Attempt all questions.

27. Two photographs are to be used as the basis for an animation. A digital camera is used to take the photographs.

(a) Describe in detail how an image is captured and converted into a digital format by the camera.

3

(b) Each frame in the completed 12 second animation is held as a GIF with a resolution of 640 × 480 pixels. The animation has a frame rate of 24 frames per second.

Calculate the file size of the animation before compression. State your answer using appropriate units. Show all working.

4

(c) The animation is tested on different computers and the colours displayed in the animation vary slightly.

(i) State which software technique could reduce this colour variation problem.

1

(ii) Explain how this technique reduces this colour variation problem.

2

(d) The animation files are compressed using LZW. Describe how the *LZW compression technique* compresses files.

2

Marks

SECTION III

PART C—Multimedia Technology (continued)

28. A DJ has connected a record turntable to his computer to transfer tracks from his vinyl record collection to his computer.

(a) Describe **one** function of the *sound card* **during** the transfer of the data to the computer.   1

(b) The DJ wants to store the tracks with no loss of sound quality.

State a suitable file format for storing the tracks without losing sound quality.   1

(c) Clips from several tracks are combined into a single file, but one of the clips is too quiet and another is too loud.

   (i) State the technique that should be used to solve this problem.   1

  (ii) Describe how your answer to part (i) solves the problem.   2

(d) The completed track plays for 5 minutes and is 16 bit stereo with a sampling rate of 44.1 KHz.

Calculate the uncompressed file size of this track. State your answer using appropriate units. Show all working.   3

The DJ often uses *surround sound* in his shows.

(e) Explain **one** advantage of surround sound over stereo.   2

The DJ has stored several tracks as *MIDI* files.

(f) Describe how individual notes are stored in the MIDI file format.   2

(g) Describe **one** benefit of using the MIDI file format to store tracks used with surround sound.   2

[Turn over

Marks

SECTION III

PART C—Multimedia Technology (continued)

29. The developers of a new digital video camera have to decide which communication interfaces to include in the camera.

The video camera is to be suitable for *streaming* live video.

(*a*) Explain **one** reason why a *Bluetooth* interface is unlikely to be chosen for streaming live video. **2**

(*b*) (i) Recommend the most suitable type of interface for this situation. **1**

  (ii) Justify your choice in part (i). **2**

(*c*) State why it would be an advantage to have *hardware codecs* built in to the video camera rather than loading in the software. **2**

30. A museum uses multimedia presentations to provide information about various exhibits.

The software that was used to develop the presentations has a *WYSIWYG* interface.

(*a*) Explain **two** reasons why WYSIWYG would help the developer during the implementation stage. **2**

All of the presentations include links to video clips. The video clips are stored in either *MPEG* or *AVI* format.

(*b*) Describe how files are stored in the MPEG format. **3**

(*c*) AVI does not allow compression but has been chosen for some short clips that are displayed in small windows.

Explain why the AVI format is suitable for storing these video clips. **2**

Some of the presentations are made available for downloading from the museum website.

(*d*) (i) Explain why a *container file* would be used to store the presentations. **2**

  (ii) Describe **one** problem that may be encountered when using a container file. **1**

To improve the display of the presentations, the museum upgrades the *graphics cards* on its computers.

(*e*) Other than converting signals, state **two** ways a graphics card assists the processor when displaying graphics. **2**

Marks

SECTION III

PART C—Multimedia Technology (continued)

31. The logo shown is stored as an *object oriented* graphic.

The logo appears in a variety of sizes on both printed documents and monitors.

(*a*) Describe **two** advantages of storing the graphic in *object oriented* format rather than *bitmapped* format.　　2

One object in the logo is a circle. The circle is altered so that it is shown in 3D.

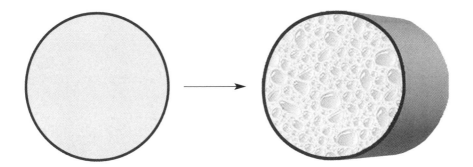

(*b*) Name **two** additional attributes that require to be stored to create the 3D representation shown.　　2

(*c*) Name a suitable file format for the 3D logo.　　1

(50)

[END OF SECTION III—PART C]

[END OF QUESTION PAPER]

[BLANK PAGE]

[BLANK PAGE]

X206/301

NATIONAL QUALIFICATIONS 2011	FRIDAY, 3 JUNE 9.00 AM – 11.30 AM	COMPUTING HIGHER

Attempt **all** questions in Section I.

Attempt **all** questions in Section II.

Attempt **one** sub-section of Section III.

Part A	Artificial Intelligence	Page 10	Questions 17 to 20
Part B	Computer Networking	Page 14	Questions 21 to 24
Part C	Multimedia Technology	Page 18	Questions 25 to 28

For the sub-section chosen, attempt **all** questions.

Read all questions carefully.

Do not write on the question paper.

Write as neatly as possible.

Mark

SECTION I

Attempt all questions in this section.

1. State the largest whole number that can be stored as a 10-bit positive integer.   1

2. Name and describe a method for measuring the performance of computers.   2

3. Data storage compensates for differences in speed between computers and peripherals. This is achieved through *buffering* and *spooling*.

    (*a*) Explain the difference between buffering and spooling.   2

    (*b*) Compensation for differences in speed between the computer and peripherals is one function of an *interface*. State **two** other functions of an interface.   2

4. (*a*) State the **type** of virus that may affect a computer during the start up process.   1

    (*b*) *Replication* and *camouflage* are two *virus code actions*. State **two** other virus code actions.   2

5. State **one** advance in computer **hardware** that has led to the increased use of computer networks.   1

6. (*a*) Describe an example in which an image stored as a vector graphic could have a larger file size than if the same image was stored in a bitmapped format.   2

    (*b*) A bitmapped graphic has a *bit-depth* of 24 bits and a *resolution* of 300 dpi.

       (i) State the number of colours that may be represented in this graphic.   1

       (ii) State the effect that increasing the bit-depth will have on the file size of the graphic.   1

7. *Analysis* is the first stage of the software development process.

    (*a*) Name the document produced at the end of the analysis stage.   1

    (*b*) Explain why the production of this document could be an *iterative* process.   1

Marks

SECTION I (continued)

8. *Pseudocode* is a design notation often used during the software development process.

   (*a*) Pseudocode should include *data flow*. State the purpose of data flow.   **1**

   (*b*) Other than data flow, state **two** benefits to a programmer of a design written in pseudocode.   **2**

9. State what is meant by the term "boolean variable".   **1**

10. Software is usually written using *subprograms*. Two types of subprogram are *procedures* and *functions*.

    (*a*) State how the use of subprograms increases the *maintainability* of a program.   **1**

    (*b*) Readability of code affects maintainability. Other than using subprograms, state **one** way to improve **readability** of code.   **1**

    (*c*) Explain **one** difference between a procedure and a function.   **2**

11. A program contains three variables, of **the same type**, with the following values:

variable1	variable2	variable3
8	4	84

    The program is written in a new language called SQAM. It contains the line of code shown below. The symbol ? represents a particular operation.

    variable3 = variable1 ? variable2

    (*a*) The value 84 is assigned to **variable3**. State the single common operation carried out by the ? symbol.   **1**

    (*b*) State the *data type* that must have been used for **all three** of the variables.   **1**

12. A *macro* can be used within application software to automate a task.

    (*a*) Name the *type* of programming language used to create macros.   **1**

    (*b*) Other than saving time, for example during writing or testing, state **two** further benefits of using macros.   **2**

    (30)

[END OF SECTION I]

Mark

SECTION II

Attempt all questions in this section.

13. Paula buys a new laptop computer which has 4 Gigabytes of *main memory* and 12 Megabytes of *cache* memory.

    (a) State **two** differences between main memory and cache memory. 　2

    (b) The computer has a **maximum** addressable memory of 16 Gigabytes. Its *address bus* width is 32.

        (i) Calculate the width of the *data bus*. 　3

        (ii) State why computers do not come with the maximum addressable memory installed. 　1

        (iii) State the effect that adding **one** new line to the address bus would have on the maximum addressable memory. 　1

    (c) Describe the function of each of the following in a memory *read* operation:

        • address bus.

        • data bus.

        • control lines. 　3

    (d) The laptop computer has several *utility programs* including a *disk defragmenter*.

        (i) State what is meant by the term "utility program". 　1

        (ii) Fragmentation of the hard disk decreases the performance of the computer. Explain why performance decreases. 　2

    (e) The laptop computer has anti-virus software. State an *anti-virus software detection technique*. 　1

Marks

SECTION II (continued)

14. Murray Components is a small business that sells computer hardware. They have a shop that employs four people.

(a) Networks can be set up as either *peer-to-peer* or *client server*.

(i) In terms of data backup, describe **one** difference between a peer-to-peer network and a client server network. 2

(ii) Murray Components have a peer-to-peer network with four workstations. Describe **one** reason why they may have chosen a peer-to-peer network. 2

(b) Murray Components is advised that a *ring topology* is not the most suitable topology to use for their LAN.

(i) Draw a **labelled** diagram of a ring topology. 2

(ii) State a more suitable topology and state **one** advantage it has over a ring topology. 2

(c) Murray Components requires a network printer to print advertising leaflets.

(i) State **two** technical requirements that should be considered when selecting a suitable printer. 2

(ii) State **two** roles of the *operating system* and describe how each is used to ensure that data is printed correctly. 4

(d) State **one** function of a *print server*. 1

(e) Murray Components starts to sell much more *solid state* storage. State **two** reasons why solid state storage is becoming more popular. 2

[Turn over

Mark

SECTION II (continued)

15. RightIT, a software company, is currently developing a cash machine program for a bank. The cash machine will offer five options to customers.

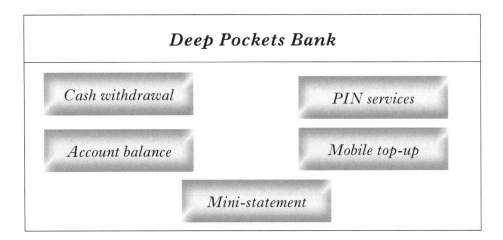

(a) RightIT decided to use an *event-driven* programming language to write the software. State **two** reasons why an event-driven programming language is suitable for this software.   2

(b) (i) State **one** other type of programming language RightIT could have used for this software.   1

　　(ii) Justify why it would also have been suitable.   1

(c) The options selected during a day are stored as a list. The bank would like the software to calculate the number of times the **mobile top-up** option appears on this list. Use pseudocode to design an algorithm to carry out this calculation.   4

(d) Once the software has been written RightIT carries out *systematic* testing. Explain how systematic testing is carried out.   2

(e) The bank is anxious that RightIT also carries out *comprehensive* testing on the software. State what is meant by comprehensive testing.   1

(f) The final version of the software is ready to be distributed to the bank. A *compiler* is chosen as the most suitable translator. Explain why a compiler is suitable at this stage.   2

(g) Several months after the software has been in use, the bank asks RightIT to include another option in the menu. This option should allow customers to withdraw cash in Euros. Name the **type** of *maintenance* required and justify your answer.   2

Marks

SECTION II (continued)

16. Sidney is an experienced programmer. He decides to write a book called "The Good Programming Guide".

(*a*) Chapter one of the book is entitled "Characteristics of a well written program". Two characteristics of a well written program are *reliability* and *efficiency*.

   (i) Define the term "reliable".   **1**

   (ii) Explain **one** way in which a program can be written to make it efficient in terms of **processor** usage.   **2**

(*b*) A well written program should make use of *parameter passing*.

   (i) State the **purpose** of an *in parameter*.   **1**

   (ii) State the **purpose** of an *out parameter*.   **1**

(*c*) Chapter two of the book is entitled "Being a team player". Sidney is keen to emphasise that on most projects there will be a team of programmers writing the software. Describe **one** example of how a programming team can ensure they will work together effectively.   **2**

(*d*) Another chapter is entitled "Saving time whilst programming". A *module library* will save programmers time as they will not have to code or test these modules independently. State **one** further benefit of making use of a module library.   **1**

(*e*) When working with data, the use of *1-D arrays* can save time.

   (i) State **two** characteristics of a 1-D array.   **2**

   (ii) Data can be stored using individual variables or using a 1-D array. Describe how the use of a 1-D array can save time when writing a program compared to several individual variables.   **2**

(*f*) Sidney sets a short programming challenge at the end of each chapter. One of these programs involves identifying a computing term from another computing related word. For example, "ram" from "program".

   Using code from a programming environment with which you are familiar, show how you would extract the term **"ram"** from **"program"**, when "program" has been assigned to the variable called "word".   **2**

(60)

word
program

[END OF SECTION II]   **[Turn over**

[BLANK PAGE]

SECTION III

Attempt one sub-section of Section III.

Part A Artificial Intelligence   Page 10   Questions 17 to 20

Part B Computer Networking   Page 14   Questions 21 to 24

Part C Multimedia Technology   Page 18   Questions 25 to 28

For the sub-section chosen, attempt *all* questions.

Mark

SECTION III

PART A — Artificial Intelligence

Attempt all questions.

17. An "intelligent" computer system has been designed to compete against people on a televised quiz show. A human presenter reads out a question and the contestant quickest to respond gets to answer the question.

Some examples of the quiz questions are shown below:

Question	Answer
What word means a water sport and also browsing the web?	Surfing
What word meaning "also" sounds like a number?	Too
Which animal is known as "the ship of the desert"?	Camel

(*a*) (i) The computer system requires the ability to process *natural language*. State **two** other aspects of intelligence involved in playing this quiz game. 2

   (ii) Explain why **this** computer system better justifies a claim of "artificial intelligence" than a chess system developed to play the world champion at chess. 2

(*b*) The first stage of natural language processing is *speech recognition*.

   (i) Name and describe the **two** other stages of *natural language processing* that the computer system will use. 4

   (ii) Describe **one** difficulty in natural language processing using the quiz questions to illustrate your answer. 2

(*c*) Speed of response is important when playing the game. Describe how **one** advance in hardware would improve response times. 2

Marks

SECTION III

PART A — Artificial Intelligence (continued)

18. A Scottish law firm is involved in the development of an expert system that will be used on the World Wide Web. The purpose of the expert system is to create legal documents after an online consultation with a client.

    (*a*) (i) Name and describe **two** components of an *expert system shell*. **4**

          (ii) The *expert system* will use *working memory* when consulting with a client. State **one** way in which information will be added to working memory during a consultation. **1**

    (*b*) Once created, the expert system will be rigorously tested.

          (i) Explain the importance of testing during the software development process. **2**

          (ii) State **two** reasons why it is important for the law firm to be involved in the testing of an expert system. **2**

    (*c*) Explain why making this expert system available online might lead to difficulties for anyone using the system. **2**

    (*d*) Describe **one** situation where a lawyer is better at providing legal documents than an expert system. **2**

    (*e*) Name and describe another real world application of an expert system with which you are familiar. **2**

[Turn over

Mark

SECTION III

PART A — Artificial Intelligence (continued)

19. The "six stones" puzzle starts with three black counters and three white counters on a board with seven spaces as shown:

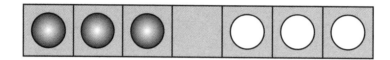

The puzzle is solved when the black and the white counters have swapped places. However, black counters can only move right and white counters can only move left according to the following four possible moves:

1. A black counter can move one space to the right into an empty space

2. A black counter can jump to the right over a white counter into an empty space

3. A white counter can move one space to the left into an empty space

4. A white counter can jump to the left over a black counter into an empty space.

(*a*) A search tree is shown below with the first move already completed.

Start State

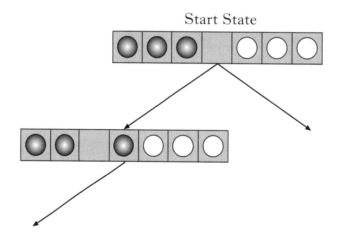

    (i) Draw the node that would be generated next if *breadth-first* searching is used.   **1**

    (ii) Draw the node that would be generated next if *depth-first* searching is used.   **1**

    (iii) Use the "six stones" puzzle to explain the term *backtracking* in depth-first searching.   **2**

(*b*) State **two** advantages of breadth-first when compared to depth-first searching.   **2**

(*c*) State another method of searching large search trees.   **1**

Marks

SECTION III

PART A — Artificial Intelligence (continued)

20. A company offers flights to various destinations stated below.

> There are direct flights from Glasgow to London and from London to Paris. Direct flights from Paris go to Rome and Seville. There is also a direct flight from Rome to Berlin.

(a) Represent the information in the paragraph above using a *semantic net*.   **3**

The company creates a knowledge base to provide information on their flights.

1.	direct(glasgow london).	*There is a direct flight from Glasgow to London.*
2.	direct(london paris).	
3.	direct(paris rome).	
4.	direct(paris seville).	
5.	direct (rome berlin).	
6.	fly_direct(P Q) IF direct(P Q).	*You can fly directly from P to Q if there is direct flight from P to Q.*
7.	one_stop(X Y) IF fly_direct(X Z) AND fly_direct(Z Y).	*There is only one stop in the flight from X to Y if you can fly directly from X to Z and fly directly from Z to Y.*

(b) Explain the term *sub-goal*.   **2**

(c) State the solutions to the query:

     ? direct(paris X)   **2**

(d) State the complex query that will determine which airport can fly to both Rome and Seville.   **2**

(e) Use the line numbers to trace the solution to the following query as far as the **first** solution.

     ? one_stop(glasgow Y)

In your answer you will be given credit for the correct use of the term *instantiation/instantiated*.   **7**

   (50)

[END OF SECTION III—PART A]

Mar

SECTION III

PART B — Computer Networking

21. A holiday park has a website on the Internet.

    Below is part of the home page for the holiday park.

(a) The *HTML* code required to create this part of the home page is shown below. Identify the **tags** represented by **A**, **B** and **C**.

```
<A>
  <head>
  <B>Bailey's Holiday Park</B>
  </head>
        <C>
        <h1>Welcome to the World of Family Fun</h1>
        </C>
</A>
```
3

(b) A software development company was appointed to create this website. State the **job title** of the person who should keep the project on track and within timescale and budget.

1

(c) The holiday park has many activities on offer such as cycling or rock climbing. There are a limited number of spaces available for each activity. The website allows guests to book and pay for these activities online before going on holiday.

 (i) Describe **one** benefit to the customer of booking these activities online.

2

 (ii) The holiday park notices that the number of activities booked has increased. State **one** possible reason for this increase.

1

 (iii) Customers are worried about the security aspect of paying online for these activities. State **one** way that the holiday park could reassure customers that paying online is safe.

1

(d) The software development company has created some web pages using *WML* code so that they can be displayed in a *WAP* browser. WML code is more limited than HTML code. State **two** limitations of WML code when creating the web pages.

2

Marks

SECTION III

PART B — Computer Networking (continued)

22. A car sales company has many branches throughout the United Kingdom. Details of all cars for sale are accessible through their *intranet*.

    (*a*) A salesperson has to download a 200 Megabyte file which is stored on the central file server. The actual file downloads at a speed of 512 kilobits per second. Calculate the time taken in minutes for this file to be downloaded using this connection. Express your answer to one decimal place. **2**

    (*b*) The *OSI* model is a set of protocols used within computer networks. State the **purpose** of the OSI model. **1**

    (*c*) Two protocols used to transmit data are HTTP and TCP/IP.

        (i) Describe the role of the IP protocol when transmitting data over an intranet. **2**

        (ii) Name **one** other protocol that could be used to transfer files across an intranet. **1**

    (*d*) When sending data across a network, *packet switching* may be used. Describe how packet switching operates. **3**

    (*e*) A *parity check* is carried out when transmitting data around a network.

        (i) Describe **one** situation where a parity check would fail to detect an error. Use an example to illustrate your answer. **2**

        (ii) Explain **one** way in which using a parity check decreases network performance. **1**

[Turn over

Mar

SECTION III

PART B — Computer Networking (continued)

23. Ti-Ket Web is a small ticket agency. Ti-Ket Web sells event tickets over the telephone or on the Internet.

    (a) (i) *"A rival company sends millions of simultaneous online requests to generate a ticket availability report for a particular concert. At this point the system is inaccessible to normal user requests."*

    Name the type of server attack described above.   1

    (ii) State **two** financial consequences of this attack on Ti-Ket Web.   2

    (iii) Describe **two** ways in which the use of a firewall could help to prevent Ti-Ket Web from further attacks.   2

    (b) Ti-Ket Web has a local area network. This network has a *switch*. Explain **one** reason why Ti-Ket Web decided to add a switch rather than a *hub* to the local area network.   2

    (c) The IP addresses for some of the devices on the network are as follows:

Computer 1	198.169.120.100	File Server	198.169.120.103
Computer 2	198.169.120.101	Router	198.169.120.104
Computer 3	198.169.120.102	Printer	198.169.120.105

    (i) State the *class* of IP address used within this network. Justify your answer.   2

    A new computer is added to the network. It is allocated the IP address **198.198.120.278**

    (ii) State **one** reason why the second octet is invalid.   1

    (iii) State **one** reason why the fourth octet is invalid.   1

    (d) *Carrier Sense Multiple Access with Collision Detection* (CSMA/CD) is used on this network to control which node can transmit at any one time. State **two** ways in which CSMA/CD might increase transmission time.   2

Marks

SECTION III

PART B — Computer Networking (continued)

24. Many families use the Internet to search for information and communicate using e-mail.

    (a) A *meta-search engine* can be used to find information on the World Wide Web.

       (i) Explain how a meta-search engine works.   3

       (ii) Name **one** method that a search engine could use to build its indexes.   1

    (b) State the purpose of SMTP.   1

    Social networking sites are used by many children to communicate with other people.

    (c) State **two** reasons why some parents may be concerned about their children accessing such sites.   2

    (d) (i) A parent has set up a *walled garden*. Explain the term "walled garden".   2

       (ii) His child uses the Internet for homework. State why the child may **not** be happy with the walled garden.   1

       (iii) An alternative method that the parent could use is "Internet filtering software". Explain why this would be more suitable for the child.   1

    (e) Some people believe that access to the Internet leads to an *Information Rich* society.

       (i) Explain the term "Information Rich".   2

       (ii) State **two** benefits of being Information Rich.   2

                                                                                 (50)

[END OF SECTION III—PART B]

[Turn over

Mark

SECTION III

PART C — Multimedia Technology

25. The logo for a new business has been drawn on paper and then scanned into a computer. The logo is shown below.

(*a*)   (i)   *CCDs* are used by both scanners and digital cameras when capturing an image. Explain how the CCD in a scanner differs from those in a digital camera.   2

(ii)   The edges of the scanned logo appeared slightly jagged. *Anti-aliasing* was used to smooth the edges. Describe how anti-aliasing achieves this.   2

(iii)   Explain how *resampling* might remove the jagged edges.   2

(*b*)   It is suggested that the logo may be stored as a vector graphic. Explain why this logo should be stored as a vector graphic rather than a bitmapped graphic.   2

Marks

SECTION III

PART C — Multimedia Technology (continued)

26. The members of the Metro Gnome Jazz Club have decided to create a club website. Members are allowed to download files; visitors can *stream* files.

(*a*) (i) Explain the term "stream". 1

    (ii) Describe **one** advantage to the Jazz Club of only allowing visitors to stream files. 2

Codecs play an important role during the streaming of files and can be implemented in hardware or software.

(*b*) A codec codes and decodes streamed files. State **two** other purposes of a codec during the streaming of a file. 2

(*c*) Explain the benefit of having codecs implemented in hardware when receiving streamed multimedia files. 2

The website includes a library of sound files stored in MIDI, WAV and MP3 formats.

(*d*) Two of the attributes stored in MIDI files are *duration* and *tempo*. Name **one** other attribute stored in a MIDI file. 1

(*e*) State **one** type of sound for which MIDI is unsuitable. 1

A particular piece of music is stored in MIDI and MP3 file formats. Both files are the same size.

(*f*) (i) Explain **one** advantage of storing files in MIDI rather than MP3 file format. 1

    (ii) A member downloads both versions of the file. Explain why the sound differs when each file is played back. 2

    (iii) State **two** ways that compression is achieved in the MP3 file format. 2

[Turn over

Mark

SECTION III

PART C — Multimedia Technology (continued)

27. David is a car racing fan. He records short video clips of races at a local circuit and transfers the clips to his computer for editing. David uses video editing software to join the video clips taken into one continuous video clip.

    (a) When he joins the clips together, David uses the *timeline* and *transition* features.

        (i) Explain why the timeline feature will be useful for David when he is producing the single continuous clip.   **1**

        (ii) Name **one** transition David could use.   **1**

    (b) One of David's video clips plays for 4 minutes. David recorded the clip using 24 bit colour with a resolution of 720,000 pixels per frame at 15 frames per second. Calculate the file size of the uncompressed video. Show all working and express your answer in appropriate units.   **3**

    (c) David stores some video clips in the MPEG file format. Describe how MPEG achieves compression.   **3**

    (d) David stores other video clips in the AVI file format. Unlike MPEG, AVI does not allow compression. State **two** reasons why the AVI format might still be a suitable file format for some video clips.   **2**

    (e) David has old analogue video recordings that he is transferring onto his computer. Describe the roles of the ADC and DSP on the video capture card during the transfer.   **2**

Marks

SECTION III

PART C — Multimedia Technology (continued)

28. Super Tutorials create multimedia lessons.

(*a*) All the lessons begin with the Super Tutorials theme tune. The tune plays for 1 minute and was recorded in 32 bit stereo using a sampling frequency of 44.1 kilohertz. Ignoring compression, calculate the file size for the theme tune. Express your answer in appropriate units and show all working. **3**

The multimedia lessons include text, video and a voice track.

(*b*) Lesson voice tracks are initially stored using the RAW file format. State the name of the **technique** used to convert the analogue signal into a digital form. **1**

(*c*) The completed lessons, which include video and voiceover sound files, are usually distributed in the RIFF file format.

  (i) The RIFF file format is an example of a *container file*. Explain the term "container file". **2**

  (ii) Explain the benefit of using container files in the distribution of multimedia files. **2**

(*d*) During testing some problems were found with the voice tracks. It was noted that some voice tracks were too loud but others were too quiet.

  (i) Name and describe the function of sound editing software which could be used to make the voice tracks play at the same volume. **2**

One voice track file also contained some unclear words. The waveform for part of this file shows the problem.

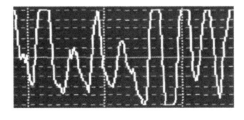

  (ii) State the term for this problem. **1**

  (iii) The problem identified in Question (*d*)(ii) may have been caused by recording at too high a volume setting. State **one** other possible reason for this problem. **1**

[Turn over for Question 28 on *Page twenty-two*

Mark

SECTION III

PART C — Multimedia Technology (continued)

28. (continued)

(e) Super Tutorials also supplies lessons on DVD. It has been suggested to Super Tutorials that *holographic* disks may replace DVDs in the future.

   (i) Describe how the physical storage of data on a holographic disk differs from a DVD.   **2**

   (ii) Holographic disks allow faster data transfer than DVDs. Explain **why** this is the case.   **2**

(50)

[END OF SECTION III—PART C]

[END OF QUESTION PAPER]

[BLANK PAGE]

X206/12/01

NATIONAL QUALIFICATIONS 2012	THURSDAY, 31 MAY 9.00 AM – 11.30 AM	COMPUTING HIGHER

Attempt **all** questions in Section I.

Attempt **all** questions in Section II.

Attempt **one** sub-section of Section III.

Part A	Artificial Intelligence	Page 12	Questions 23 to 27
Part B	Computer Networking	Page 18	Questions 28 to 31
Part C	Multimedia Technology	Page 22	Questions 32 to 35

For the sub-section chosen, attempt **all** questions.

Read all questions carefully.

Do not write on the question paper.

Write as neatly as possible.

SECTION I

Mark

Attempt all questions in this section.

1. Write the ten digit binary number **1001001001** as a positive integer.

   1

2. A computer system uses *floating point representation* to store *real* numbers.

   (*a*) State the part of floating point representation that determines the **range** of numbers stored.

   1

   (*b*) State the part of floating point representation that determines the **precision** of numbers stored.

   1

3. Ali has created a poster using *bitmapped* graphic software. Describe how a bitmapped graphic is stored.

   2

4. *Protocol conversion* and *buffering* are two functions of an interface. State **two** other functions of an interface.

   2

5. The table shows types of computer memory listed in **descending** order of *speed of access*, (fastest first). Identify the **two** missing types (1) and (3).

(1)	
(2)	Cache
(3)	
(4)	Backing store

   2

6. Audrey creates and saves a new document to the hard disk.

   (*a*) State **two** tasks carried out by the *file management* part of the operating system during this save operation.

   2

   (*b*) State **one** task carried out by the *input/output management* part of the operating system during this save operation.

   1

SECTION I (continued)   *Marks*

7. The diagram below shows the layout of a small LAN.

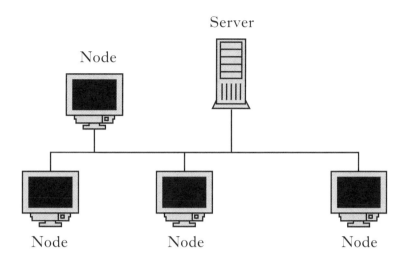

    (*a*) Name this network *topology*.   1

    (*b*) The network shown above is a *client server* network. State **one** advantage of a
          client server network over a *peer-to-peer* network.   1

    (*c*) A device is required to connect this network to the Internet. Name this device. 1

8. The software development process is *iterative*. Explain how the word iterative
    applies to this process.   2

9. Many software development projects use *top-down design*. Explain the process of
    top-down design.   1

10. Name **one** *graphical design notation*.   1

11. An *interpreter* may be used in the software development process.

    (*a*) Name **one** stage of the software development process where the interpreter
          may be used.   1

    (*b*) Explain how the interpreter is used in the stage named in part (*a*). 1

12. Describe **one** difference between a *scripting* language and a *procedural* language. 2

Mark

SECTION I (continued)

13. (a) State what is meant by a *boolean* variable.   1

(b) Explain how a boolean variable could be used in a *linear search* algorithm.   1

14. Software should be both *reliable* and *robust*. Explain the terms "reliable" and "robust".   2

15. State **one** way in which documentation produced at the *testing* stage of the software development process will be used during *corrective* maintenance.   1

16. State **two** characteristics of programming code that improve *maintainability*.   2

(30)

SECTION II

Marks

Attempt all questions in this section.

17. Tara, who works for Consumer Friend Magazine, has produced the following table.

Consumer Friend Magazine				
Processor	Clock Speed (GHz)	MIPS	MegaFLOPs	Data Bus Width (Bits)
Inrel Core Gi	3·2	72,495	63,933	64
Atheton E	2·8	73,665	63,105	64
Motorilla T	2·0	49,924	51,150	128

NOTE: One MegaFLOP = One Million FLOPs

(a) Explain why clock speed alone is not considered a good measure of **processor** performance.

1

(b) Tara states that the Atheton E is better than the Inrel Core Gi as it has a higher MIPS result. Explain why Tara may be incorrect.

2

(c) A computer containing the Motorilla T has a 32 bit address bus, a 128 bit data bus and 24 control lines. Calculate the maximum addressable memory of this computer.

Show all working. State your answer using appropriate units.

3

(d) All processors contain an *ALU* and a *control unit*.

(i) State **one** logic operation performed by the ALU.

1

(ii) Describe the purpose of the control unit.

1

(e) The manufacturers of the Inrel Core Gi are considering using a wider data bus in a new processor design. State **one** reason why this will improve processor performance.

1

[Turn over

SECTION II (continued)   *Mark*

18. A system called EarthWatch gathers data from weather stations all over the world. Each station uses a *terminal* to enter data into the EarthWatch *mainframe*.

    (*a*) Apart from the physical size or the cost of a mainframe, explain **one** difference between a mainframe with terminals and a network of computers.   2

    (*b*) The mainframe's hard disk system has been continually storing weather data for 5 years. A message appeared on the main screen stating that the data file could not be stored on the hard disk due to lack of storage space. However there is enough space on the mainframe's hard disk system.

        (i) Explain the **most likely** cause of this apparent lack of storage.   2

        (ii) Name a piece of software which could solve the problem identified in (i).   1

        (iii) State the **class** of software that the item named in (ii) belongs to.   1

    (*c*) Each EarthWatch weather station contains 10 terminals connected to a file server situated 80 metres from the terminals. State a suitable transmission medium to connect the terminals to the server. Explain your reasoning.   2

    (*d*) The EarthWatch mainframe performs many memory read operations per second. Write down the steps involved in a single memory read operation. Name the *bus* or *control lin*es involved at each step.   3

SECTION II (continued)   *Marks*

19. Harry is an expert on human linguistics. He is currently studying a **data file** on his computer containing 3000 ancient Chinese characters.

(*a*) State whether this file is an *ASCII* file or a *UNICODE* file. Explain your reasoning.   2

(*b*) Harry buys a printer to print the characters. Apart from cost, name **two** other relevant characteristics of a printer.   2

(*c*) Harry is concerned that this data file may contain a *file virus*.

(i) Explain whether Harry's concern is justified.   2

(ii) State what is meant by a computer virus.   1

(iii) State **one** action of a virus.   1

(*d*) Harry saves a picture of each character in GIF format. State **two** characteristics of the GIF format.   2

[Turn over

SECTION II (continued) *Mark*

20. Martin is a systems analyst. He has just been given a new project to work on.

   (a) (i) Explain why Martin will interview the client during the *analysis* stage. 1

   (ii) State **two** other techniques that Martin may use during the analysis stage. 2

   (b) Martin is responsible for producing a document at the **end** of the analysis stage.

   (i) Name this document. 1

   (ii) State **two** reasons why this document has to be agreed with the client before it is finalised. 2

   (c) Explain how a systems analyst could be involved in the **testing** stage of a project. 1

   (d) When Martin was at University, he earned money by being part of *independent test groups*. Explain why he cannot be part of the independent test group assigned to **this** project. 1

   (e) Effective testing of the software needs to be both *systematic* and *comprehensive*. Explain the terms "systematic" and "comprehensive". 2

   (f) Towards the end of the project, Martin is told that the project is running over budget. State the **job title** of the person who has the responsibility for the project budget. 1

SECTION II (continued)   *Marks*

21. Over the summer, a garden centre has been running a "tallest sunflower" competition.

Entrants have completed an online entry form to provide their name and the height of their sunflower. These have been collated into two lists. Samples from these lists are shown below.

Name of entrant	Height of sunflower (metres)
Eildih Brown	2·15
Helen Atkins	1·79
Mark Ames	2·32
Jenna Wylie	1·41

(a) State the *data structure* and *data type* used to store the list of heights.   2

(b) Using *pseudocode*, design an algorithm to find and display the **name** of the person growing the tallest sunflower.   6

(c) The garden centre wants to give a consolation prize to the grower of the **shortest** sunflower. A number of changes need to be made to the pseudocode you wrote in part (b).

   (i) State **one** change that you would make to your pseudocode from part (b).   1

   (ii) Explain **why** this change is necessary.   1

[Turn over

SECTION II (continued)

Mark

22. A travel agent uses a suite of software to help advertise holidays and make bookings. Part of the pseudocode that was written for the software is:

---

if cost per person is less than 500
    set band to 'cheap'
end if

if cost per person is greater than or equal to 500 AND cost per person is less than 2000
    set band to 'medium'
end if

if cost per person is greater than or equal to 2000
    set band to 'expensive'
end if

(a) By using a holiday cost per person of £495, explain why this pseudocode would not produce *efficient* code.   2

(b) Show how these lines could be rewritten in a more efficient way.   2

(c) When the above is implemented as a subroutine, state whether the variable "cost per person" would be passed by *reference* or *value*. Justify your answer.   2

Each holiday booking is assigned a unique reference code. The software which creates this code uses *concatenation* within a *user-defined function*.

(d) Explain the term *concatenation*.   1

(e) Explain the term *function*.   2

(60)

[END OF SECTION II]

SECTION III

Attempt one sub-section of Section III.

For the sub-section chosen, attempt *all* questions.

SECTION III

Mark

PART A — Artificial Intelligence

Attempt all questions.

23. The Turing Test can be used during the development of *chatterbots*.

    (a) State the purpose of the Turing Test.   1

    (b) Describe how a chatterbot attempts to have a meaningful conversation.   2

    (c) State **two** weaknesses that may be present in a chatterbot's conversation with a human.   2

    (d) State **one** improvement in processors and describe how it improves the performance of a chatterbot.   2

24. The water jugs puzzle is a well known artificial intelligence problem. In this puzzle there are two jugs; the jug on the left holds three litres and the one on the right holds five litres. Neither has any measuring markers on it. There is a tap that can be used to fill the jugs with water. The goal of the puzzle is to measure exactly four litres of water.

    A computer is used to find a solution.

    (a) State the aspect of intelligence which a computer is demonstrating when finding the solution to the water jugs puzzle.   1

    (b) Some people would argue that a computer solving this puzzle does **not** have artificial intelligence.

    State **one** reason which supports this opinion.   1

SECTION III   *Marks*

PART A — Artificial Intelligence (continued)

24. (continued)

The computer represents both jugs being empty as (0,0). The node (3,0) means that the three litre jug on the left is full and that the five litre jug on the right is empty.

It attempts to solve the puzzle by generating the following states:

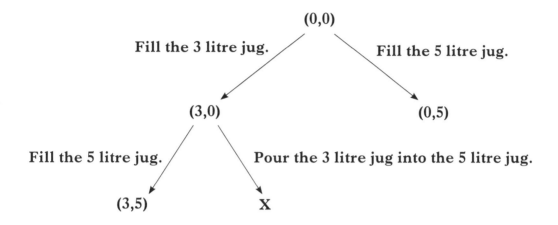

(*c*) Name this type of diagram.   1

(*d*) The order of nodes currently in memory is (0,0), (3,0), (0,5) and (3,5).

Explain which *search technique* is being used.   2

(*e*) State **two** other search techniques that could be used.   2

(*f*) State the node missing from the diagram, marked by the letter X.   1

(*g*) The diagram shows three of the possible moves:

   • Fill the 3 litre jug
   • Fill the 5 litre jug
   • Pour the 3 litre jug into the 5 litre jug.

State **two** other possible moves.   2

[Turn over

SECTION III

Mark

PART A — Artificial Intelligence (continued)

25. CeramicSee is a vision system that is used in the quality control of ceramic tiles.

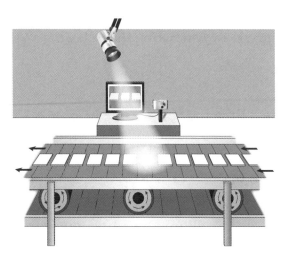

CeramicSee rejects tiles with flaws such as:

- wrong shade or colour

- physical damage such as chips or scratches.

(a) Describe **two** ways in which CeramicSee overcomes common problems with vision systems. 　2

(b) The *image acquisition* stage of CeramicSee uses a digital camera capable of 32 bit colour to capture an image of a tile. Calculate the maximum number of different colours in an image. 　1

(c) Name and describe **two** other stages of computer vision. 　4

(d) CeramicSee uses an *artificial neural system* to identify defective tiles. Describe how *weights* are used in the **training** of an artificial neural system. 　3

(e) State **another** example of an application that uses an *embedded* vision system. 　1

SECTION III

Marks

PART A — Artificial Intelligence (continued)

26. Intelligent robots are one application of artificial intelligence. This has resulted in the development of robots for household tasks particularly floor cleaning.

Floor cleaning robot

(*a*) State what is meant by the term "artificial intelligence".

1

(*b*) State **one** characteristic of an intelligent robot when compared to a dumb robot.

1

(*c*) Describe **two practical** difficulties associated with the development and use of an intelligent robot for floor cleaning.

2

(*d*) (i) State **one** legal implication of the use of an intelligent robot.

1

(ii) Explain how a manufacturer of robots can address legal implications.

1

[Turn over

SECTION III

Mark

PART A — Artificial Intelligence (continued)

27. An online multi-player game has been created. Each player in the game is a character such as a troll or an orc that can acquire various objects as they move through the game eg a sword or armour. A character can only defeat another if they have the correct object.

    This knowledge base stores the current state of the game:

    1. has_found(troll jewel).   *The troll has found a jewel.*
    2. has_found(troll sword).
    3. has_found(orc armour).
    4. has_found(druid potion).
    5. has_found(druid lance).

    6. is_weapon_against(lance troll).   *The lance is the weapon to use against a troll.*

    7. is_weapon_against(sword orc).
    8. is_weapon_against(jewel troll).

    9. life_points(troll 1000).   *The troll has 1000 life points.*
    10. life_points(orc 200).
    11. life_points(druid 140).

    12. stronger_than(X Y) IF life_points(X A) AND   *Character X is stronger than character Y if X has life point A and character Y has life points B and A is greater than B.*
        life_points(Y B) AND
        A>B.

    13. can_defeat(X Y) IF has_found(X Z) AND   *Character X can defeat character Y if character X has found item Z and Z is the weapon against character Y and character X is not character Y.*
        is_weapon_against(Z Y) AND
        not(X=Y).

    (a) State the solution to the following query:

        ? has_found(X potion)   1

    (b) State the query required to find the weapons that can be used against the troll.   2

SECTION III   *Marks*

PART A — Artificial Intelligence (continued)

27. **(continued)**

    (*c*) Explain how the following query would be evaluated:

        ? not(life_points(troll 800))   2

    (*d*) Trace the **first** solution to the query:

        ? can_defeat(troll Y)

        In your answer you will be given credit for the correct use of *backtrack*.   8

    (*e*) The original software specification stated that a player can defeat an opponent
           if the player has found the appropriate weapon for that opponent and that they
           are stronger than the opponent.

        (i) The existing rule 13 must have **one** line added to meet this requirement.

            can_defeat(X Y) IF has_found(X Z) AND
                              is_weapon_against(Z Y) AND
                              not(X = Y) AND
            ┌─────────────────────────────┐
            │ .... │
            └─────────────────────────────┘

        State the missing line of the new rule.   2

        (ii) State the **type** of maintenance that this change to the software is best
              described as.   1

                                                                          (50)

[END OF SECTION III—PART A]

[Turn over

SECTION III

Mark.

PART B — Computer Networking

Attempt all questions.

28. It is important that computer networks are designed to agreed standards, such as the Open Systems Interconnection (OSI).

    (a) (i) State the name of the *layer* of the OSI model at which a *router* functions. **1**

        (ii) State the name of the *layer* of the OSI model that carries out *data encryption*. **1**

    (b) *TCP/IP* is a set of protocols used in network communication. State the actions carried out by the **IP** part when transmitting data over a network. **2**

    (c) Explain how *CSMA/CD* improves network performance. **2**

    (d) The byte of data below is transmitted across a network. It contains a *parity* bit.

    ### 1000 1111

    State which **kind** of parity was used when sending this data. Justify your answer. **2**

    (e) Data can be sent *synchronously* or *asynchronously*. State which of these methods uses start and stop bits and how it uses them. **2**

SECTION III

Marks

PART B — Computer Networking (continued)

29. A local dentist has created a cabled network to connect his four computers and a printer.

   (*a*) Explain why the dentist chose to use cables rather than wireless to connect the network.

       1

   (*b*) The dentist is worried that a hacker may get access to his patient files without his knowledge. Name the **type** of attack that the dentist is worried about.

       1

   A website is being created for the dentist using *HTML* as shown below.

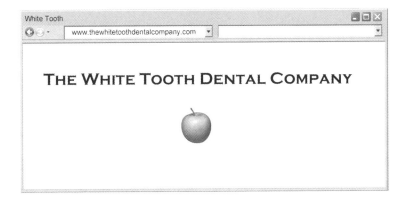

   (*c*) Write the HTML code for the **title tag** of this webpage.

       2

   (*d*) The apple image displayed on the web page was captured in *true colour*. State what is meant by "true colour".

       1

   (*e*) The website is published on the Internet. However, the dentist realises that search engines are not finding his website.

     (i) State an additional element that should be included in the HTML code in order to help a search engine find the website.

       1

     (ii) Name the section of the HTML code in which this element should be placed.

       1

   (*f*) The dentist would like the website to be viewed on mobile phones. The *HTML* code will have to be re-written in a different language.

     (i) Name the language required to create webpages for mobile phones.

       1

     (ii) State the protocol that allows mobile phones to access the website.

       1

     (iii) State **one** other type of device that uses this protocol.

       1

   (*g*) After testing the mobile phone version of the website, an error was found. State the type of *maintenance* required to fix errors not identified during testing.

       1

SECTION III

Mark

PART B — Computer Networking (continued)

30. A teacher requires a username and password to give her remote access to her school server.

(a) Other than *TCP/IP*, name a protocol which could allow remote access to a server.   1

(b) The school's server has been subjected to a *denial of service (DOS) attack*.

   (i) Describe **one** possible denial of service attack.   2

   (ii) State **two financial** implications for the school as a result of this DOS attack.   2

(c) The school's server has a *firewall*. State **two** ways that a firewall could be used to monitor access to the school network.   2

(d) Hacking is a **security** issue that the school will have to consider. Other than a firewall, describe **two** software methods that the school could employ to try to prevent hackers from gaining unauthorised access to their server.   4

(e) The school is concerned about accidental or malicious loss of data from their server. They have installed a *mirror disk*. Explain how a mirror disk would help them in this situation.   2

(f) The school is concerned about staff and pupils accessing websites from school computers.

   (i) Explain how a *walled garden* would prevent staff and pupils from accessing unsuitable websites.   2

   (ii) Describe **one** way that *Internet filtering* software differs from a walled garden.   1

(g) The teacher creates a *WPAN* to connect her laptop, printer and smartphone. Explain **one** reason why a *WPAN* would be appropriate for this network.   1

SECTION III

Marks

PART B — Computer Networking (continued)

31. A sports centre has a local area network of 10 computers and 2 printers.

(*a*) Explain why *class A IP addressing* is **not** suitable for this network.   1

(*b*) A network interface card is required to provide a physical link to the local area network. The network interface card contains a *MAC* address. Describe the purpose of a MAC address.   1

(*c*) When data is transmitted across the network a *Cyclic Redundancy Check* (CRC) is carried out. Describe how the **receiving** device uses CRC.   3

(*d*) The sports centre has a website which allows bookings to be made and paid for online. Members have expressed some security concerns about using their credit cards to pay for bookings online.

   (i) Explain how *packet switching* would increase the security of the transmitted data.   2

   (ii) The sports centre's network can also set up a direct communications link to their head office. State the method of switching which would set up this direct link.   1

(*e*) The sports centre has an *ADSL* connection to the Internet.

   (i) The manager wants to download a 150 Megabyte file. The ADSL connection has a download speed of 8 Megabits per second. Calculate the time taken to download this file. Show all working.   2

   (ii) When the file was downloaded it took longer than the time calculated in part (i). Suggest **two** reasons for this increase in download time.   2

(50)

[END OF SECTION III—PART B]

[Turn over

SECTION III

Mark

PART C — Multimedia Technology

Attempt all questions.

32. Peter is a guitar teacher who uses his website to give pupils access to audio files. The audio files are instrumental tracks for practice between lessons.

    (*a*)   (i)   The audio files are stored in the *MIDI* format. One benefit of this file format is its small size. State **two** other benefits of using the MIDI file format.

2

           (ii) MIDI files are stored using *sound attributes* such as *duration* and *tempo*. Describe the terms "duration" and "tempo".

2

    (*b*) State **two** reasons why the pupils may prefer the *MP3* file format to the MIDI file format.

2

Peter has demonstration video clips on his website.

    (*c*) The video clips were originally taken using a resolution of 1024 × 768 with a frame rate of 25 fps. Calculate the file size of an uncompressed 24 bit video clip which plays for 64 seconds. Show all working. State your answer in megabytes.

3

Pupils must *stream* the video clips to their computer when viewing.

    (*d*) Peter is worried about breach of copyright. Explain how **streaming** will help avoid this.

1

    (*e*) Assuming there are no hardware or software problems, explain why streamed video may pause when viewed on a pupil's computer.

2

SECTION III

Marks

PART C — Multimedia Technology (continued)

33. EasyVid manufactures video cameras. The EasyVid Super4 digital video camera will be a new digital video camera designed to replace the current EasyVid Power3 digital camera.

EasyVid Power3

4·1 megapixels
Bluetooth & Firewire enabled
40 Gb hard disk
Video editing software supplied

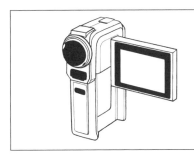

EasyVid Super4

12 megapixels
Bluetooth & USB 3·0 enabled
Built-in hardware codecs
Built-in 3 in 1 card reader
Video editing software supplied

(a) State **two** advantages USB 3·0 has over Firewire.   2

(b) It had been suggested that the EasyVid Super4 should be WiFi enabled. The manufacturer decides **not** to add a WiFi interface. State **one** reason other than cost to support their decision.   1

(c) The EasyVid Super4 has no hard disk. Explain why using removable solid state storage would extend battery life.   2

(d) The manufacturer has built in hardware *codecs* to the EasyVid Super4. Describe **one** advantage and **one** disadvantage to the user of a hardware codec rather than a software codec.   2

(e) Video editing software is provided with both cameras. This includes *transition features*.

   (i) Explain what is meant by a "transition feature".   1

   (ii) Name and describe **one** effect usually available as a transition.   2

(f) Explain why neither camera uses an *ADC* during data transfer to a computer.   1

[Turn over

SECTION III   *Mark*

PART C — Multimedia Technology (continued)

34. The Bestview Camera Club has an annual photographic competition. Presentation software is used to display the entries as a slide show.

    (a) A design technique suitable for planning the presentation is storyboarding. Describe **two** features of a storyboard that should be included in the design of the presentation.   2

    Spoken comments about entries are to be recorded for inclusion in the slide show.

    (b) Calculate the **uncompressed** file size of an 8 bit, 24 second stereo recording sampled at 11 kHz. Show all working. State your answer in appropriate units.   3

    The WAV file format is used to store the spoken comments. WAV files are compressed.

    (c) (i) State the name of the compression method used.   1

        (ii) Describe **how** this method achieves compression.   2

    (d) Describe how the file size of a spoken comment could be significantly reduced without changing the sampling depth.   1

    A short musical introduction is used at the start of the slide show. Figure 1 shows the waveform of the introduction. Figure 2 shows the waveform after an effect has been applied.

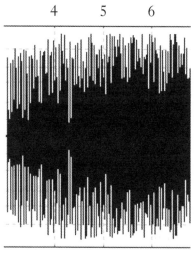

Figure 1

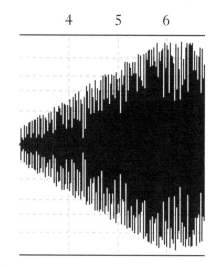

Figure 2

    (e) State the effect applied to the sound.   1

SECTION III

Marks

PART C — Multimedia Technology (continued)

34. (continued)

(f) During testing of the slide show, it is noted that one audio file has been *clipped*.

(i) Explain the term "clipping". You **must** include a diagram in your explanation.

2

(ii) Describe how *normalisation* would have avoided the problem of clipping.

2

(iii) Describe **one** disadvantage of normalisation.

2

[Turn over for Question 35 on *Page twenty-six*

SECTION III

Mark

PART C — Multimedia Technology (continued)

35. A designer has stored a graphic in each of *GIF*, *PNG* and *SVG* formats.

(a) The designer notices that adding each circle to the graphic increases the file size of the SVG file but **not** the GIF or PNG files. Explain why the SVG file size increases.

2

(b) The finished graphic will be displayed on a variety of screen sizes. Explain why SVG might be the **best** format to choose in this situation.

2

(c) Part of the code for the smallest circle is changed from **rgb(0,78,0)** to **rgb(0,16,0)**. Describe the effect of this change on the circle.

2

(d) Dithering can be used with the GIF file format but is unnecessary with PNG.

   (i) Explain the term *dithering*.

1

   (ii) Explain why dithering is not required for the PNG file format.

2

(e) The graphics software used by the designer includes *anti-aliasing*.

   (i) State the purpose of anti-aliasing.

1

   (ii) Describe a situation when anti-aliasing might have to be used.

1

(50)

[END OF SECTION III—PART C]

[END OF QUESTION PAPER]

SQA HIGHER COMPUTING
2008–2012

SECTION I

1. (a) (i) *Any one from:*
   - An <u>array/grid</u> of pixels
   - Each dot/pixel has a <u>binary value</u>
   - Each pixel stored as a bit/byte/binary value/black=1 & white=0

   (ii) *Any one from:*
   - As a number/list of objects (each of which has attributes defining the objects)
   - <u>Objects</u> are defined by attributes
   - An example object can be used to describe eg rectangle and attributes

   (b) *Answer:* Bit-mapped
   Justification: any one from:
   - Composed of grid of (individual) pixels
   - Does not contain/is not comprised of (collection of discrete) objects
   - It is pixelated
   - It is a photograph/taken with a digital camera

2. (a) • It looks for a suspicious pattern of behaviour (which was previously associated with a virus)
   - Accept use of a valid example to illustrate concept

   (b) *Any one from:*
   - A trojan horse is not self replicating
   - Does not infect other files

3. −74

4. (a) *Any one from:*
   - Returns the CPU/processor to its initial state
   - (Saves contents and) clears registers

   (b) The address is sent <u>from the processor</u> to memory only

5. (a) *Any one from:*
   - Disk editor/clean up
   - disk recovery tools
   - backup
   - emulator

   (b) *Any one from:*
   - Arranges data block contiguously (together) *(one mark)* speeding up the access time *(one mark)*
   - Gathers free space together *(one mark)* reducing access time *(one mark)*

6. (a) (i) A is a ring
   (ii) B is a star

   (b) B, Star

7. *Any one from:*
   - No fractional part/decimal stored
   - Stored as a 'whole' number

8. (a) *Any two from:*
   - reliability
   - robustness
   - portability
   - efficiency
   - maintainability
   - user interface
   - readability

   (b) It revisits earlier stages of the software development process (in the light of new information)

9. (a) *Any two from:*
   - Increased productivity/saves time (since the task will be completed faster than choosing menu choices, dialogue boxes etc.)
   - Customisation of the package by creating your own menu commands/buttons to automate common search/sort
   - Ability to perform complex tasks recorded by another user (with higher skill level)
   - Less chance of human error

   (b) Scripting language

10. Declarative

11. (a) Pseudocode

    (b) In: pounds
        In: euros

    (c) By reference.
    Explanation: any one from:
    - the value passed into the subroutine, (changed) and passed back out
    - the variable itself is passed in and out
    - the dataflow states that it is an out parameter

12. *Any two from:*
    - Performs decision or selection
    - Involving two or more choices
    - Avoids the use of multiple or nested If statements
    - Increases clarity/readability

SECTION II

13. (a) (i) *Any one from:*
    - Increase the width of the data bus *(one mark)* - more data fetched from memory in each F/E cycle *(one mark)*
    - Increase the amount of cache memory *(one mark)* reduces access to slower RAM *(one mark)*
    - Increase the number of registers *(one mark)* more fast access storage within the CPU *(one mark)*
    - Install faster access hard drive *(one mark)* reduce time taken to load/save data *(one mark)*
    - Install dual processors *(one mark)* to increase throughput of instructions *(one mark)*

    (ii) *Any one from:*
    - Overheating of processor
    - Physical limitation of other components such as switching speed of memory, speed of data bus, etc

    (b) (i) *Any one from:*
    - FLOPS – counts the number of floating point operations per second
    - Application based tests – measure the actual time taken to perform a practical task

    (ii) *Any one from:*
    - Tests used are real-world uses/related to the actual tasks done by the customer
    - Are not dependent on one hardware feature of the computer

(iii) *Any one from:*
  - Measure actual work done by the processor
  - Independent of instruction complexity/ word size/application task

(c) 2^{32} x 64 **or** 2^{32} x 8

= 274877906944 bits = 34359738368 bytes

= 32 Gb

(d) Each location has a unique binary address

14. (a) (i) *Answer:* A is the router
  Justification: any one from:
    - used to connect the LAN to the Internet
    - used to connect LANs to telecommunication lines
    - used to direct packets using IP address
  (ii) *Answer:* B is the hub
  Justification: any one from:
    - used on LAN to connect stations
    - cheap method of connecting station to a LAN
    - does not require complex routing at this level

(b) (i) *Any one from:*
  - Upgrade/install a switch instead of a hub
  - Upgrade/install cables with a higher bandwidth
  - Upgrade/install network cards which support higher bandwidth
  (ii) *Any one from:*
  - (Upgrade/install a switch instead of a hub) as signals are directed to individual station rather than all stations reducing network traffic
  - (Upgrade/install cables with a higher bandwidth capability) increasing data transfer rate
  - (Upgrade/install network cards which support higher bandwidth) increasing data transfer rate

(c) Web server **or** proxy server

15. (a) Input/output (management system/function)

(b) (i) gif only supports 256 colours **or** uses 8 bit colour **or** has a limited range of colours
  (ii) Bmp **or** jpeg **or** png **or** tiff

(c) 6 x 8 x 1200 x 1200 x 24

= 1658880000 bits = 207360000 bytes

= 197·8 Mbytes

(d) Status signals

(e) *Any one from:*
  - Serial printer can send data over a longer cable/greater distance
  - Serial does not suffer from skew

(f) *Any one from:*
  - High Resolution (of at least 1200 dpi) – to match the resolution of the scanned image
  - High bit depth (of at least 24 bits) – to match the scanned image
  - (larger) buffer – as the print jobs are large/photos have large file size
  - correct interface – to connect to James's computer
  - speed of <u>printing</u> (ppm) – may want to print a number of photos/large photo quickly

(g) *Any two from:*
  - Image must be edited at pixel level
  - Each pixel in the image will have to be edited to match surrounding pixels
  - No (discrete) objects to manipulate

16. (a) *Any two from:*
  - Amount of (available) RAM/memory
  - Minimum clock speed/powerful processor
  - Processor type
  - Version of OS
  - Identify peripherals required.
  - Sufficient storage capacity

(b) *Any two from:*
  - Sections of code can be assigned to different programmers
  - Modules can be tested individually
  - Easier maintenance as more readable
  - Availability of module library
  - Individual modules can be amended/replaced

(c) *Any one from:*
  - mid(winner,1,3)
  - left(winner,3)
  - winner.substring(0,3)
  - concat(winner[1,winner[2],winner[3])
  - winner[1]+winner[2]=winner[3]
  - winner[1:3]

(d) (i) array *(one mark)* of real/single/float *(one mark)*
  (ii) There are a number of expressions of the algorithm:

Set fastest to first time in list
Loop from 2 to 8 [for rest of array items
  If array(current)< fastest then
    Set fastest to array(current)
  End if
End loop
	Set fastest to 1 000 000 [number over range]
	Loop 8 times or each array item
	  If array(current)< fastest then
	    Set fastest to array(current)
	  End if
	End loop

Set fastest to 1
Loop from 2 to 8 [for rest of array items]
  If array(current) <array(fastest) then
    Set fastest to current
  End if
End loop
	In summary, 1 mark for each of the following:
	• Setting initial value
	• Loop (with end) for traversal of array
	• Comparison of current element with min value (with end if)
	• Assignment of new min value

(iii) Each time the fastest is reassigned, set a position variable equal to the loop counter (Set fastest to current).

17. (a) (i) *Any two from:*
  - Liaise with client and project team
  - Investigates current system
  - Observe workplace
  - Writes the software specification
  - Allow requirements elicitation techniques

  (ii) *Any two from:*
  - Results in a legal document for which both client and company are accountable
  - Software specification informs all future stages
  - Software specification validates future stages
  - Saves wasted time and effort designing and creating software which is not what client wants

(b) (i) *Any two from:*
  - Uses a range of data types
  - Sequence of control instructions

- Similar control structures such as selection (if etc) and repetition (loops)
- Both are modular

(ii) • Has specialised routines for event handling, creation of windows/buttons etc
- Applications with a graphical interface are suited to code being activated by events

(c) (i) A set of pre-written/pre-tested subroutines/functions/code (for use in the development of software)

(ii) *Any one from:*
- Local variable can only be seen/accessed in the module of code in which it is created
- Create local variable
- Use parameter passing

(iii) *Any two from:*
- Variables cannot be accidentally altered by other parts of the program
- Variables will not conflict with variable with the same name in other modules
- Aids maintainability
- Aids modularity

(d) *Any two from:*
- Testing all of the individual modules independently
- Testing modules work together
- Acceptance/beta/field testing
- Use an independent test group

(e) *Any one from:*
- Customers will have a range of hardware ie various types of TVs and various set-top boxes.
- The software will be required to run on a variety of hardware other than the one it was designed on.

(f) Adaptive maintenance *(one mark)* – since it is the environment that is being changed *(one mark)*

SECTION III

Part A – Artifical Intelligence

18. (a) *Any two from:*
- Need human control to stop damage to walls/robot etc
- Need control to force examination of items of interest along the tunnels
- Unknown items so limited vision recognition to aid navigation
- Uncertain/no route map (for path planning)
- Humans can decide/choose/control path

(b) *Any two from:*
- Power supply: battery or umbilical cable
- Ability to move over surface if uneven (legs, wheels or caterpillar track)
- Processor power/light sources to cope with vision systems
- Potential return of artefacts
- Ability to move in sloping tunnels
- Small physical size to allow navigation of small tunnels
- Ability to turn round/reverse in dead end tunnels
- Robust/ruggedised to cope with terrain/damage

(c) (i) *Any one from:*
- Stops in front of an unidentified obstacle/ detects danger
- If control is broken or Rover develops a fault
- Where Rover has to make independent choices
- Learning a route/creating an internal map

(ii) *Any one from:*
- Emergency stopping (in front of an unidentified obstacle)
- It can navigate back to control room (if control is broken or Rover develops a fault)
- It can choose shortest/safest route between two points
- Any other valid application of intelligence to described situation

(d) Perfective

19. (a) *Any two from:*
- Totally different style of game available eg simulation
- More complex (realistic) graphics/higher resolution
- Improved user interface/interactivity
- Multiplayer games
- Games will play strategies/show intelligence
- Games will have realistic sounds
- Greater variety of input devices available

(b) *Any two from:*
- Availability of event driven languages rather than programming in machine code
- Specialised graphics routines
- Better software development tools eg dedicated/graphics module libraries, error reporting tools, compiler/interpreters
- Rapid development environments
- Complex data types and file handling routines built in to languages

(c) (i) *Any two from:*
- Different actions can be processed simultaneously
- A specific example eg character moving, change of sound effect
- Faster image rendering/3D graphics etc
- Ability to evaluate multiple strategies and select best
- Faster response to user input/actions

(ii) *Any two from:*
- Increased memory (RAM/ROM)
- Faster processors
- Increased cache
- Better, more varied input/output devices
- Improved graphics cards empower higher resolution monitors
- Better sound card for improved audio
- Improved graphics cards/more video RAM
- Faster peripherals (hard disk access rates)

(iii) *Any two from:*
- Increased memory to hold larger and more complex programs
- Faster processors to manipulate data faster
- Increased cache to reduce time taken for fetch/execute cycle
- Varied input devices to give more realistic experience eg sensors in controller
- Higher resolution monitors to display clearer images
- Improved audio for better sound effects (eg surround sound)
- Improved colour depth for realistic graphics

20. (a) (i) LISP
(ii) Prolog
(iii) functional (code is common LISP)

20. (b)

21. (a) (i) *Any one from:*
    - Unclear as to what 'it' refers to
    - Which side is "it" to be put on
    (ii) Ambiguity as to which pyramid to move, choice of two available

(b) The word "grip" might not be in SHRDLU's dictionary/ memory/program

(c) *Any one from:*
    - Formal languages have small vocabulary/ NLP has to cope with 'millions' of possible words
    - Formal languages have clearly defined and unambiguous words/NLP is subject to colloquialisms, ambiguity etc
    - Formal languages use strict grammar/NLP accepts deviations

(d)
    - Natural language understanding
    - Natural language generation

(e) *Any two from:*
    - Extracts keywords from user input
    - Uses a bank of responses suited to the keyword
    - Generates an appropriate response
    - Uses a generic response if no suitable response found

22. (a) (i) any of lines 1 to 7
    (ii) line 8 **or** line 9

(b) • depth first
    • breadth first

(c) A=11, Y=collins

22. (d) match at line 9 with X instantiated to 'conrad' and Z instantiated to 'bean'
    first sub-goal is apollo(A, conrad, _, bean)
    match at line 4 with A instantiated to '12'
    return to line 9, second sub-goal is crew_landed_on_moon (12) match at line 8 with first sub-goal apollo(12, , ,) match at line 4
    return to line 8 with second sub-goal A>10 (which gives 12>10) which is true
    return to line 8 with third sub-goal not(A=13) which gives 12=13 as false so the sub-goal is true
    solution to query is true

(e) The query returns the answer false but they did walk on the moon.
    The order of names in the query is the wrong way round.

SECTION III

Part B – Computer Networking

23. (a) Save on the cost of laying the cables/digging up school grounds

(b) • Lots of users, potential for a very busy central line with lots of collisions in a bus – star reduces this
    • Channel failure in a star will not affect the entire network

(c) Class B

(d) *Any one from:*
    • Will have insufficient addresses for each of the devices on the network
    • Many addresses will go unused

(e) *Any one from:*
    • Compares the originating IP address to a list of IP addresses it will accept data from
    • Decides whether the port that the data is using is appropriate

(f) *Any one from:*
    • To protect the pupils whilst they are online.
    • By only allowing access to permitted web sites/do not access unsuitable materials

24. (a) *Either:*
    <title>Mel's Website</title>
    Or:
    <title>Mel's Website </title>

(b) • Queries other search engine
    • Groups the responses

24. (c) • Web pages can now include a range of multimedia elements/Higher resolution graphics available
    • As the time taken to download these elements has been reduced

(d) *Any two from:*
    • Splitting the file into packets
    • Adding a sequence number to each packet
    • Re-assembling the packets at the destination

(e) (i) Application layer
    (ii) Presentation layer

(f) Changes to one layer do not impact upon the other layers

25. (a) *Any two from:*
    • Code is already written
    • Code already tested
    • Code already documented

(b) • Two clocks are not synchronised/machines are working independently/no timing mechanism required
    • Each byte of data requires a start and stop bit

(c) *Any one from:*
    • Packets do not have to follow same route
    • So each packet takes the most efficient route
    • Improving network performance
    • Security may be improved as individual packets are intercepted rather than whole message/file

(d) (i) *Any one from:*
    • Where an even number of bits have changed from origin to destination, eg 11111111 changed to 11111100 during transfer

- Where sender and receiver are using different parities, eg 11111111 (even parity) changed to 11111101 during transfer but receiver working under odd parity
  (ii) Cyclic Redundancy Check/CRC
  (iii) *Any one from:*
  - Performing a calculation at origin and send result with data
  - Perform (same) calculation at destination and comparing the answers

(e) *Any one from:*
  - Extra time is taken to perform error checking tasks (increasing transfer time)
  - Reduces the number of transmission errors that go undiscovered (improving performance)
    or
  - Extra data is sent eg checksum/parity (increasing transfer time)
  - Reduces the number of transmission errors that go undiscovered (improving performance)

26. (a) *Any two from:*
  - The DNS converts the URL into an IP address
  - DNS looks up URL on database to find related IP
  - IP establishes which web server/device hosts the file

(b) • Incorrectly entered URL/URL not valid
  - This particular URL to IP mapping is not present on this DNS

(c) (i) *Any one from:*
  - Through satellite connection
  - Through electricity cables
  - Mobile broadband
  (ii) *Any two from:*
  - Need to authenticate the user
  - Need to ensure user permissions are set correctly
  - Need to ensure that data is not intercepted during transmission
  (iii) *Any two from:*
  - Use a "callback" facility to ensure correct phone line being used
  - Encrypt data giving each employee a restricted key
  - Use a secure protocol such as HTTPS
  - Allocate minimum necessary access to each user

(d) (i) *Any two from:*
  - Mobile phone
  - Palmtop/PDA
  - Music/MP3 player
  - Digital (still or video) camera
  - printer/headphones
  (ii) *Any two from:*
  - Save clutter of cables
  - To exchange data between them (eg from camera to computer)
  - Synchronise information on devices (eg address book)

(e) (i) Regulation of Investigatory Powers Act
    Note: Not "RIPA" or RIP Act
  (ii) *Any two from:*
  - Checking Internet history
  - Access decryption keys/encrypted data
  - Undercover officers/surveillance

SECTION III

Part C – Multimedia Technology

27. (a) *Any two from:*
  - Typical users
  - Hardware requirements
  - Software compatibility
  - Multimedia components
  - Inputs/outputs/boundaries
  - Functions/features
  - Budget
  - Timescale

(b) • Use of timeline to synchronise events which are happening simultaneously
  - Use of scripting to control objects on screen

(c) *Any two from:*
  - Check that all links are correct/go to correct location
  - Check that all media elements play correctly

(d) (i) *Any two from:*
  - Do not need to obtain/find/download/ buy viewer
  - Do not need to check compatibility of other viewers
  - Player software will take less space in backing storage than the software used to create the application
  - Player software will not take as much processor time as the software used to create the application
  - Player software will use less memory than the software used to create the application
  - Do not need to buy expensive software used to create the application
  (ii) *Any one from:*
  - No need to test application with other viewers
  - User cannot edit the application

(e) Multimedia elements (video/sound) require much processing to compress/process/display Powerful/fast processors enable this to happen within real time/reasonable time

(f) Stores data in a number of 3D images *(one mark)*
    Hundreds of images may be saved in different layers/full depth of medium *(one mark)*

(g) *Any one from:*
  - Real or 3D display technology – user can engage with an object/situation, gain more info through added depth
  - Increased capacity of RAM – more video/sound can be held while editing/processing
  - Firewire/USB – easy connection of hardware eg digital video camera, and fast access times
  - High resolution monitors – allow high definition video
  - Graphics card – onboard processor for video allowing main processor to do other tasks

28. (a) *Any one from:*
  - The RGB colour code for each colour used in the image is stored in the colour lookup table
  - A local palette storing the selection of colours used in the image

(b) *Any one from:*
  - Changes to the palette affect the whole screen at once, so faster than editing pixel by pixel
  - Can be used to produce special effects which would be much slower to produce by updating pixels

(c) (i) anti-aliasing
  (ii) *Any two from:*
  - Simulates extra resolution
  - Blurs/smooths the edge
  - By changing colour of pixels along the jaggy edge

(d) (i) Transparency/opacity
(ii) GIF, PNG

(e) (i) (Areas of a particular colour) compressed by storing the colour to repeat *(one mark)* and the number of pixels to repeat for *(one mark)*

(ii) The image does not contain that many large blocks of the same colour *(one mark)*
Therefore the amount of compression will be limited *(one mark)*

(f) (i) As the complexity of the image/number of objects increases the file size increases *(one mark)* A bitmap image will have a constant file size, regardless of complexity *(one mark)*

(ii) VRML/WRL – plain text file of individual object descriptions/stores objects and their attributes

29. (a) (i) *Any one from:*
    - Data is played as it is received
    - Playing a remote file

    (ii) *Any one from:*
    - Do not want visitors to have to wait for the complete video to download.
    - Do not want user to have a copy of the video file

    (b) 15 fps x 3 bytes x 600 x 800 x 120 seconds
    /1024/1024/1024 = 2·41 Gigabytes

    (c) *Any one from:*
    - Embedded font should have been used
    - Make the font available to download

29. (d) (i) ADPCM
    (ii) Saves the difference between each sample, to reduce amount of data to be stored. A valid description of compression will be allowed if it matches candidate's answer to (i)

    (e) *Any one from:*
    - Take less storage space
    - Mono quality is adequate for speech

    (f) *Any two from:*
    - Media elements could be copied from website and used without permission
    - Media elements could be edited without permission and distributed
    - Media elements could be sold as user's own material

30. (a) *Any one from:*
    - Sound is sampled (captured) at regular intervals
    - Converting <u>analogue</u> into digital form

    (b) (i) No background noise as data is digitally created and stored
    (ii) *Any one from:*
    - All individual notes/instruments can be edited/have affects applied
    - Accept an example of an attribute that could be edited eg tempo
    - Can be edited as a text file.

    (iii) *Any two from:*
    - Does not contain vocals
    - Not as realistic as digitised sound
    - Can depend on quality of sound card
    - Artist values interpretation/skill level/ performance

    (c) *Any two from:*
    - *Fade:* used to prevent abrupt starts and stops, may be applied to vocals at the end of a track
    - *Normalising:* digitised sound is stretched to use full dynamic range available, to make sound clearer
    - *Echo:* give effect of a large area, may make choir sound as if they are in a church
    - *Resampling:* change the frequency of the sample rate

COMPUTING HIGHER 2009

SECTION I

1. (a) *551*

   (b) 10110111

2. *Any one from:*
   - Unicode can represent all character based alphabets **or** ASCII has a very limited character set
   - Characters can be user/software defined **or** ASCII does not allow user defined characters

3. 24

4. (a) *Any one from:*
   - Allows the user to directly edit contents of disk sectors/blocks
   - Allows user to get/remove file fragments
   - Allows recovery of damaged/deleted blocks/files

   (b) To (locate and) load the rest of the OS at startup

5. *Any one from:*
   - Not spread by infecting other files or self replicating
   - Disguises itself or appears to be a harmless/ordinary/useful file

6. *Any one from:*
   - Fewer fetches required from slower main memory/RAM/cache
   - Access to data in registers is faster than to RAM or cache

7. (a) *Any one from:*
   - Unable to run on available OS
   - Clash with existing software

   (b) *Any one from:*
   - Lack of available memory
   - Less powerful/unsuitable processor
   - Unsuitable graphics/sound card

8. (a) *Any one from:*
   Server controls a function of entire client-server network
   In peer-to-peer, control is distributed not centralised

   (b) *Any one from:*
   - Easier to do backups with centralised file server
   - Better security of data (through multi-level access/password & usernames)
   - Software servers allow better control of licensing/upgrades/remote installation

9. JPEG achieves <u>greater</u> compression, therefore less time to be transferred/reduction in net traffic
   or
   JPEG (more) widely compatible, as several versions of TIFF exist

10. *Any two from:*
    - Stages are revisited/repeated
    - As a result of new information/information gained later in the process
    - In order to improve the solution

11. *Any two from:*
    - States boundaries & scope of problem
    - Fix timescale and total budget of project
    - States <u>exactly</u> what the software is required to do
    - Used as a reference during the rest of the stages of the process
    - Informs testing by outlining test criteria

12. (*a*)

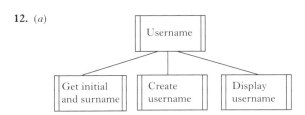

(*b*) Concatenation

13. *Any one from:*
- To make an application more flexible/more usable by a larger group of users
- Allows experts to customise/extend the functionality of the application
- Allows experts to automate the functionality of the application
- Allows beginners to perform tasks beyond their level of expertise
- Creating/editing a macro

14. *Any one from:*
Client **or** Programmer **or** Document/Technical writer **or** Project Manager

15. (*a*) Program can cope with unexpected input/conditions without failing

(*b*) *Any one from:*
- Software performs as predicted on duplicated test runs
- Software will not stop due to design flaws
- Output is correct for all specified inputs

16. A new item of hardware is installed which the program must interact with

17. (*a*) A collection/group of pre-written/pre-tested sections of code (which can be used within programs)

(*b*) • created within this program by the programmer, not already present/presupplied
- module has a value/which returns a single value to a program

SECTION II

18. (*a*) *Any two from:*

- Processor halts the current process/task
- Processor stores current state/register values
- Clears (internal) registers
- Loads a new task/temporarily passes control to another routine.

(*b*) Max memory $= 2^{24}$
$= 2^4 \times 4$ Mb
$= 16 \times 4$ Mb
$= 64$ Mb

(*c*) • Address bus is set up with the address to be written to
- Data bus is set up with data to be written
- Write (control) line is activated
- Data on data bus is placed in memory location specified by address bus

(*d*) File management:
Any one from:
- update file allocation table
- locate location of data blocks for storing/updating file
- protect existing files from overwriting

I/O management
Any one from:
- coordinate transfer of data (to flash card)
- check readiness of flash card for data transfer
- detect transmission errors
- buffer data in transit.

(*e*) *Any one from:*
- Security software included on flash card
- Speed of access has improved
- Reduction in physical size (ie mini-SD cards)

19. (*a*) Computer Misuse Act

(*b*) (i) *Any one from:*
Checksum **or** Memory Resident Monitoring **or** Heuristic Detection

(ii) *Any one from:*
- Checksum – reports when calculations on a file produce varying results between initial storage and subsequent openings
- Memory Resident Monitoring – check for suspicious actions/activity in memory (copying/deleting files, program modification)
- Heuristic Detection – search for code that activates at a specific time/action
  - searches for exe files
  - writes to disk other than in normal OS procedures
  - rates files/actions according to level of threat

(iii) *Any one from:*
- Adding (dummy) instructions
- Changing the order of instructions

20. (*a*)

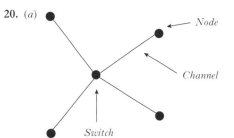

(*b*) *Any one from:*
- Channel failure in star will only affect 1 node
- Channel failure in bus will affect all nodes

(*c*) Switch directs signal to appropriate node **or** hub broadcasts to all nodes therefore less network traffic
or
Switch can use full bandwidth to send signal **or** hub bandwidth is shared reducing possible collisions

20. (*d*) *Any one from:*
- Server queues/organises print jobs
- freeing processors of other nodes for other tasks
- central control of print queues maximises (efficiency of) hardware usage

(*e*) *Any two from:*
- use of tabs to hold several pages open at once
- site adviser to rate relevance/reliability/security of sites
- spell checking built in
- search box built into browser window, removes need to go to search page
- predictive text/drop down on search criteria
- micro-browsers on palmtops etc

21. (*a*) *Any one from:*
- Data conversion (serial/parallel, analogue/digital)
- Handling status signals (ready/busy)
- Voltage conversion (peripherals typically work at higher voltage, needs to be reduced to CPU voltage)
- Protocol conversion (differences in data sizes/speeds require handling)

(b) (i) Serial transfers signals down a single line bit by bit

Serial transfer of 1011

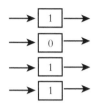

(ii) Parallel transfers groups of bits simultaneously down several lines

(c) *Any one from:*
- Fewer errors over longer distances (as a result of skewing)
- Transmission possible over longer distances
- Skewing does not occur

22. (a) Event-driven

Program is waiting for an event/action from the customer to respond to

or

Procedural
- a sequence of instructions with clear start and end point
- program will be modular, making use of procedures/functions

(b) *Any two from:*
- Maintenance is helped by improved readability
- Modules can be allocated to programmers to work on simultaneously
- Testing can be carried out at module level first, reducing errors later
- Errors are more easily traced in a modular structure
- Use of parameters/local variables in modules avoids unexpected variable changes in other parts of code

(c) (i) Systematic

(ii) Comprehensive

(d) Set over3 = 0
For each car that day
  If duration >180 then
    Add one to over3
  End if
End loop

(e) Visual Basic: Println formatNumber(percent,2) **or** picdisplay.print(format(percent, "#.00"))

TrueBasic: PRINT "The percentage is";
    PRINT USING "#####.##" : percent

Comal: PRINT USING "#####.##" : "The percentage is"; percent

Pascal: writeln('The percentage is', percent:5:2)

(f) Perfective maintenance as they are adding a new function not in the original software

23. (a) Real/float/single/currency

(b) (i) Amount or category not to be changed by this module, so only current value passed in

(ii) Cost
This is calculated by the module and updated, the amended variable being passed back out

(c) (i) Whole program

(ii) *Any two from:*
- Increases modularity, reducing unexpected clashes between variable names
- Increases portability, can re-use without changing variable names
- Makes data flow clear, so improving readability
- Makes data flow clear, so improving maintainability

(d) *Any one from:*
Greater range of hardware platforms means
- the larger the potential sales market
- a greater risk of potential hardware/software conflicts
- more able to deal with future upgrades by/for customers

(e) (i) Each discrete/separate IF in the series will be checked even after the match is found
Nested if will only be executed until a condition is true (then it will exit the statement)

(ii) CASE statement

(f) (i) *Any two from:*
- Data type
- Number of elements/size of array
- First index/start and end (both start and end would <u>imply</u> no. of elements)

(ii) Does not take up memory storing a second copy of the array
or
Does not waste processor time making a second copy of the array

SECTION III

Part A – Artificial Intelligence

24. (a) Turing test

(b) *Any one from:*
- Only tests one aspect of artificial intelligence
- Depends on the intelligence or personality of the user/interrogator
- Test is text-based

(c) (i) *Any one from:*
- Use humour/jokes
- Ask questions dependent on previous answers/repetition/contradiction
- Bring in topical information

(ii) *Any one from:*
- Humour is too sophisticated/high level for computers
- Computer may not store all previous answers/be able to cross-reference between answers/no common sense
- Computer may not have been updated with current events/knowledge base may be too narrow

25. (a) *Any two from:*
- Auto-translation
- Speech driven software/speech recognition
- NL search engines
- NL database interfaces

(b) (i) Sentence can be understood in a number of ways/different meanings/interpretations.

(ii) *Any one from:*
- Unclear what the 'it' refers to – broken window or broken bottle
- Was the food international or were they international specialists

(c) Natural Language Understanding

(d) (i) Natural Language Generation

  (ii) Difficult to generate a correct response without coming to an understanding of the meaning of a sentence

(e) *Any two from:*
  - Changing nature of language/new words or usage of words eg test, surf
  - Inconsistencies in grammar. eg There is a number of books in the box/There are a number of books in the box.
  - Similar sounding words eg through/threw **or** similar spelling eg lead the pack/lead piping

26. (a) *Any one from:*
  - Narrow area/field of knowledge/topic (bicycles/one manufacturer's bikes)
  - Clear boundaries/well-defined.
  - Advice would be clearly defined based on certain inputs (probability/uncertainty is limited)

(b)

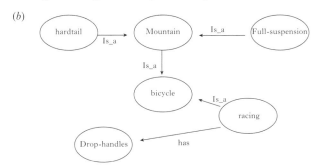

(c) (i) *Any one from:*
    Inference engine selects appropriate facts or rules/uses pattern matching to search for a solution based on user input.
    or
    User interface accepts user responses via suitable interface (such as radio buttons, list boxes) & outputs advice

  (ii) Knowledge base

(d) *Any one from:*
  - Support for the existing software ie expert system shell has been used before
  - More robust as components are pretested
  - Lower level of programming skill required

27. (a) LAEIOURN

(b) (i) LAUREN

  (ii) LEN

  (iii) *Any one from:*
    - Search only stores current path (LEN)
    - When the leftmost branch has been exhausted and it backtracks to L
    - Redundant nodes (AUR) are removed/previous path not saved

(c) (i) Each node has a large number of descendants causing the number of nodes to become huge very quickly.

  (ii) Rubik cube, backgammon, Go, draughts

  (iii) *Any two from:*
    - A heuristic indicates which of the descendant nodes is more promising/where a solution is likely to be
    - through the use of an evaluation function/calculation
    - making the need to visit every node less likely/cutting down the search space

  (iv) *Any one from:*
    - Faster selection/comparison of descendant nodes
    - Faster calculation of evaluation functions which rate the node

(d) Algorithm/fact/rule/code/state likely to be contained in cache reducing need to fetch <u>from slower main memory</u> **or** causing faster execution of fetch-execute cycle

28. (a) (i) X=bird
        X=platypus

  (ii) subclass(X, mammal)

(b)
  - Match at 7, Y is instantiated to egg_laying, <u>Y = egg_laying</u> (is output/solution)
  - Match at 8, X is instantiated to platypus, <u>subgoal subclass(platypus,Z)</u>
  - Match at 2, Z instantiated to monotreme, <u>subgoal has(monotreme,Y)</u>
  - Match at 8, X instantiated to monotreme, <u>subgoal subclass(monotreme,Z)</u>
  - Match at 1, Z = mammal, <u>subgoal has(mammal,Y)</u>
  - Match at 5, Y instantiated to liveyoung, <u>Y=liveyoung</u> (is output/solution)

(c) *Any one from:*
  - The two answers ("egg laying" and "live young") are conflicting
  - Platypii do not bear live young

(d) Recursion/Recursive (rule) **or** Inheritance (rule)

SECTION III

Part B – Computer Networking

29. (a) (i) Class C
        Any one from:
        - the first 3 octets are fixed
        - the first octet is between 192-223
        - the first octet is 193, which is in the range for class C

  (ii) 249
       Class C can have 254 nodes/there are 5 used leaving 249

(b) (i) Any valid answer relating to the reduced performance of Node 1 on LAN 1 eg
      - The hard drive on LAN 1 may be fragmented
      - Node 1 on LAN 1 may have other devices connected …printer/scanner
      - Node 1 LAN may have more software installed
      or
      Network related responses
      - The stations on LAN 2 may be configured with a higher bandwidth
      - The network software/hardware on LAN 2 may be more efficient/newer version than LAN 1
      - There may be less traffic on LAN 2 than LAN 1

  (ii) *Any one valid justification which matches answer to part (i)*
      - Fragmented drive- takes longer to retrieve/store data from the drive slowing performance
      - More devices requires more system resources reducing performance
      - More software installed requires additional system resources reducing performance
      - Higher bandwidth means data will be sent/received in less time
      - More efficient network software may reduce time taken for data to be sent/received
      - Reduced traffic will allow more bandwidth to stations transmitting

(c) They all use a common/standard network protocol/OSI

(d) SMTP

(e) • The message is broken into packets
   • Each packet is given a sequence number/(sequence) header
   • The message is reassembled at the destination

(f) • Sender performs a calculation and sends result/CRC with the data
   • Receiver recalculates the result/CRC and compares it to the result/CRC sent
   • prompt to resend if no match/if results match accept packet/error if no match

(g) • The router takes the destination IP/logical address from the packet
   • and matches this with the MAC/physical address of the node

30. (a) A – Highland Chess League
   B – Welcome to the Highland Chess League Home Page
   C – Play the board <u>not</u> the man

(b) To upload his website/pages/files

(c) (i) • To describe the contents/purpose of the site
      • To enable a search engine to select websites according to these keywords

   (ii) A spider collects data/keywords (from meta tags) and it is stored in a database/index

      Answers include:
   (iii) • Results of search depends on how accurately gathered data represents content of site
      • A meta search engine may gather the results of searches from other search engines
      • Sites may be rated/ordered to indicate popularity/relevance
      • Sponsored links may be included in results pushing more relevant sites down the list

(d) (i) • the Domain Name Server (DNS) tried to match the given URL
      • to find the corresponding IP address
      • the IP could not be found/the DNS has no record of the URL

   (ii) Register the domain name

31. (a) Systems analyst

(b) (i) *Any two from:*
      • No need to change the infrastructure of the building.
      • Not limited by the number of users logging on
      • More economical than the cabled solution
      • Less additional hardware required
      • Customers able to sit where they like/wireless laptops give more portable network access

   (ii) ISDN, ADSL or cable modem

(c) *Any one form:*
      • Many people logged on in the coffee shop sharing the same Internet connection
      • Internet is very busy at these times so less external bandwidth

32. (a) *Any one from:*
      • They have software and hardware permissions/rights which are denied the other users
      • They belong to a group with advanced/higher/different permission rights

(b) (i) Passive attack

(ii) <u>Description of</u> Encryption: data is coded before being sent making it unreadable if it is intercepted

(c) Backup happens ***after*** the disaster and disaster avoidance attempts to **prevent** it happening

(d) (i) *Any one from:*
      • The differential backup process will take less time than a full backup
      • The backing storage requirements are lower than that of a full backup
      • The performance of the network will be affected for a reduced duration

   (ii) *Any one from:*
      • Restore of a differential backup takes more time than a full restore due to the number of files changed
      • If differential backup is done too many times the number of layers make it slower/larger than a full backup
      • Accept any reasonable scenario which shows the above to be true

(e) (i) Internet filtering is where access to a web page is denied/filtered due to properties of page eg content, file type, URL, key rating

   (ii) A walled garden allows access to only those websites that have been specifically chosen

(f) *Any two from:*
      • The students need access to the whole Internet and not simply a restricted part of it
      • The walled garden may not have the most recent research sites whereas filtering allows this
      • Any answer relating to restriction of walled garden to all but permitted list
      • Filtering method is more versatile than the walled garden (in blocking vulgar/illegal sites to different groups)

(g) *Any one from:*
      • Packet filtering – data packets are filtered depending on IP or TCP content
      • Circuit (level) filtering – a secure connection is set up between the source and network denying access to packets outwith the secure connection

(h) (i) Data integrity is ensuring that the data is correct/up to date

   (ii) Data security is making sure that only authorised users have access to the data

SECTION III

Part C – Multimedia Technology

33. (a) (i) *Any one from:*
      • DSP allows the hardware encoding of data stream
      • DSP allows high speed manipulation of video data eg compressing the video as MPEG

   (ii) Digital video cameras have replaced analogue video cameras therefore there is no need for video capture card as the video can be transferred directly to the computer.

(b) (i) $\underline{2 \times 60 \times 10} \times \underline{1000 \times 800 \times 24}$
      = 23040000000 bits
      23040000000 / 8 = 2880000000 bytes
      2880000000 / 1024 = 2812500 Kb
      2812500 / 1024 = 2746.6 Mb
      2746.6 / 1024 = <u>2.68 Gb</u>

   (ii) The frame rate is too low at 10 fps (and should be increased to 25 fps)

(iii) • Sequencing
• Transition

(c) It contains more than one media type within the one file (audio and video)

(d) • Use of key frames (I-frames)
• (Between key frames) only changes to the frames recorded
• Each frame compressed (as JPEG)

34. (a) *Any one from:*
• WYSIWYG – would require faster processing speed as it has to process higher resolution graphics and a more complex interface
• WYSIWYG – would require a larger RAM as the software would need to display and manipulate higher resolution graphics
• WYSIWYG – would require a higher resolution monitor to display the high resolution graphics

(b) • Reflected light is detected by the (linear) CCD/light sensitive elements/light sensors
• It is converted to an analogue electrical signal
• The ADC converts this to a digital signal

(c) (i) Re-sampling/increasing resolution

(ii) *Any one from:*
• Increases number of pixels, looks at surrounding pixels and gives best guess at what the output pixel colour should be
• Bilinear interpolation/Output pixel values calculated from weighted average of pixels in the nearest 2-by-2 group
• Bicubic interpolation/Output pixels are an average of the surrounding pixels by weighting the value of the pixel in the average based on its distance from the origin pixel. Pixels farther away have less effect on the resulting pixels value than its nearest neighbours.

(iii) Run Length Encoding (RLE)
Repeated pixels of the same colour can be stored using the colour of a pixel followed by the number of times it occurs eg seven black pixels could be stored as the number pair

(d) (i) *Any one from:*
• Sounds that can't be heard by the human ear are not encoded
• Sounds that are drowned out by other sounds are not encoded
• Compressed using Huffman algorithm/encoding
• Low frequency sounds are sampled at a lower resolution

(ii) *Any two from:*
• Has a smaller file size than MP3 so can be downloaded faster/uses less memory/backing storage
• Individual instrument data stored so a single instrument can be edited at a later date
• Flexible/universal format so no need for additional CODECs
• MIDI is universal format so can be embedded directly into the web page

35. (a) *Any one from:*
• VRML
• WRL

(b) SVG stores the **attributes** of the graphic (rather than the actual picture itself)

(c) *Any one with two attributes from:*

Object	Suitable Attributes include:
circle	cx, cy, r, stroke, stroke-width, fill
rect	x, y, width, height, fill, stroke, stroke-width
text	x, y, font-family, font-size, font-weight, fill, stroke

(d) (i) It is blue,

(ii) • 8-bits used to store colour intensity of **each** of RGB (in range 0 to 255)
• Triad of RGB stored in 3 x 8 = 24 bit colour

(e) • A 2D image mapped onto the surface of a 3D object
• A graphic 'pasted' onto the surface of a 3D object

(f) *Any one from:*
• GIF
• MNG (animated version of PNG)

36. (a) (i) *Any two from:*
• Storyboard/Timeline
• A diagrammatical representation of each slide
• Details of each of the multimedia objects and their attributes
• Details of navigation structure

(ii) *Any two from:*
• Greater control over the timing of events
• Use of variables
• Flexibility over user interface
• May contain scripting language
• Ability to control external devices

(b) (i) • 30 x 22000 x 8 = 5280000 bits
• 5280000 / 8 = 660000 bytes
• 660000 / 1024 = 644.53125 = 644.5 kilobytes

(ii) (512 x 1024) / 644.53125 = 813 (or correct answer using figure from part (i))

(iii) *Any one from:*
• Uses less power so can work from batteries
• More robust as it has no moving parts

(c) (i) ADPCM has a smaller file size than PCM

(ii) *Any one from:*
• ADPCM stores the differences between the samples (rather than the actual samples themselves)
• Uses 4 bits to store the changes between samples rather than the 16 bits for each sample

(d) Voice recording has been clipped/highest & lowest frequencies removed

(e) (i) • No need to connect the phone with cables
• Other valid

(ii) *Any one from:*
• Slower data rate
• Less secure
• Other valid

(f) *Any one from:*
• Where there used to be separate devices for making phone calls and playing MP3 files, the smart phone combines both of these functions in the one device
• Where there used to be separate devices for making phone calls and voice recordings, the smart phone combines both of these functions in one device

(g) (i) Information can be stored in layers (throughout the full depth of the medium)

(ii) Information can be read a layer at a time (in Parallel) rather than as a sequence of bits

COMPUTING HIGHER 2010

SECTION I

1. -45

2. (a) The virus waits until a condition is met
   - before it triggers/is activated/performs its task
   - or example of condition eg Date reached, access to Internet
   (b) *Any one from:*
   - Replication
   - Camouflage
   - Delivery

3. • An instruction (to be executed)
   • Data (to be processed)

4. *Any one from:*
   - To store data that has been passed from the computer processor (while it waits for the printer to process it)
   - Acts as a buffer
   - Allows computer processor to carry on with other tasks
   - Any other suitable description

5. 2. Read line is activated **or** Read signal is sent
   4. Instruction is decoded and executed

6. (a) • Copyright Designs and Patents Act
   (b) *Any one from:*
   - The files he shares are copyrighted
   - Not his files to share
   - He does not have permission to make the copies
   - He only has one licence
   - Financial loss to company as a result of reduced sales
   - Any other suitable

7. *Any one from:*
   - LAN will use dedicated (cable or wireless) media and a WAN will use telecommunication systems
   - LAN media owned by the organisation, WAN owned by communication companies
   - LAN tends to be uniform in its type of connection/cable, WAN tends to use more than one type of transmission medium
   - Any other valid difference with explanation

8. *Any one combination from:*
   - Each connected node on a switch receives full bandwidth – Nodes on a hub share the bandwidth
   - Data sent to single/addressed/required node with switch – A hub broadcasts to all nodes
   - Reduction/avoidance of collisions when using a switch – Use of a hub increases network traffic

9. (a) A number with fractional part/floating point number/decimal number
   (b) Array of Boolean

10. (a) *Any one stage and reason from:*
    - Implementation – Program must be planned to show how program is to be coded
    - Testing – Used to create test data/To help identify errors
    - Evaluation – Design is used to ensure that all requirements in software specification are met
    - Documentation – Design is used as a template for the creation of the technical description of the code
    - Maintenance – Design will be looked at and changed to match the maintenance required
    (b) *Any two from:*
    - Breaks problem into smaller problems
    - Continuing to break down sub problems
    - Until they can be solved easily/trivially/simply

11. (a) *Any one from:*
    - (Structured) listing
    - Printout/hardcopy of program/source code
    - Source code
    (b) *Any one from:*
    - Provides a record of work done (required by project manager/client)
    - Aids maintenance (by keeping a record of changes made)
    - Track staff changes within the development team
    - Accept a purpose of a specific type of documentation, such as purpose of User Guide, Technical Guide, Internal Documentation
    - Any other valid
    (c) *Any one from:*
    To give advice on:
    - how the parts of the program work
    - the memory/processor/system requirements/specifications
    - potential software/hardware clashes
    - the version/maintenance history
    - Other valid

12. (a) *Any one method and reason/effect from:*
    - If compiled version of program is used, meaning translator is not needed during execution
    - Use of local variables where possible, allowing memory to be reused when it goes out of scope
    - Software is modular/has no unnecessary code/variables, saving on memory used for duplicate/unnecessary code
    - Variable types should be appropriate for data for example using integer as opposed to real to save memory
    - Any other valid method and effect/reason
    (b) • Software can run on any other platform/processor/"type of computer" **or** other than the one it was designed for with little or no change

13. *Any one from:*
    - Automate complex or frequently used task
    - Writing macros
    - Customising user interface
    - Increase/extend functionality
    - Any valid response

SECTION II

14. (a) Bootstrap loader
    (b) (i) • Data format conversion – Converting the photograph data from serial to parallel or vice versa (as used in the computer system)
        • Handling of status signals – The camera will send signals to say it is ready to send data
        (ii) *Any two from:*
        - Voltage conversion
        - Protocol conversion
        - Buffering/data storage
        - Any other valid
    (c) (i) *Any two from:*
        - Reduce the file size
        - Fewer bits per pixel
        - Faster download
        - Smaller storage on disk/RAM
        (ii) Fewer possible colours available (or any other valid), so poorer quality pictures.
        (iii) • 4 × 6 × 600 × 600 pixels
              • 8640000 × 16 bits
              • (= 138240000) = 16.48 Mb
    (d) • Memory management – locates the file in main memory
        • Input/Output – controls the moving of (blocks of) data (between main memory and hard drive)

(*e*) *Any one from:*
- Faster access times allows almost instant reviewing of pictures
- Small and lightweight allowing small camera size
- No moving parts so silent/robust
- No moving parts so less battery power required
- Less battery power so more pictures can be taken on one charge

(*f*) *Any one from:*
- JPEG is lossy whereas GIF is lossless
- GIF only has 256 (8 bit) possible colours, JPEG can have 16.7 million (24 bit)
- JPEG requires less backing storage or memory than the equivalent GIF, hence is faster to transmit
- GIFs can be animated whereas JPEGs are not (like any graphic format can only be used within animation)
- GIFs allow transparency whereas JPEGs don't (because they are a single layer)
- Other valid

15. (*a*)
- 2^{32} possible locations
- 64 bits per location
- $2^{32} \times 64$ bits = 32Gbytes

(*b*) *Any one from:*
- Cache has faster access time than main memory speeding up fetching
- Holds frequently used instructions speeding fetching
- Wider internal bus speeding up data transfer
- Physically closer to processor speeding up transfer
- RAM in cache is made up from fast static RAM rather than slower dynamic RAM speeding access times
- Holds pre-fetched instructions in cache instead of accessing slower main memory

(*c*) *Any one from:*
- Compatibility with the operating system to allow software to run/install
- Sufficient RAM/memory/Backing Storage/Processor to satisfy minimum program requirements/to enable it to run
- Any other valid with justification

(*d*) (i) *Any one from:*
- MIPS measures processor throughput and are independent of other computer components ie hard disk speed
- ABTs depend on performance of other components and therefore may rate identical processors differently
- MIPS measures processor throughput whereas ABTs measure the entire system
- Other valid answer with explanation

(ii) FLOPS **or** Clock Speed

(*e*) *Any one from:*
- Each computer has its own backing storage and does not rely on central server
- No complex server software to set up so easier to create shared area of peer-to-peer
- Any other suitable

16. (*a*) String

And any one from:
- "Jun" is textual and must be a string
- Number data types cannot accept text
- String operations to be carried out

(*b*) Substring

(*c*) Case month of
When "Jan"– Set month to "01"
When "Feb" – Set month to "02"

(*d*) Concatenation

(*e*) 8 bits per character
= 8 * 6 = 48 bits or 6 bytes

(*f*) (i) *Any two from:*
- Follows a sequence of instructions/defined start and end point
- Use of subprograms/functions
- Range of variable types
- Program control using repetition and selection structures
- Uses arithmetical and logical functions
- Any other valid

(ii) *Any one from:*
- Code activated/order of execution assigned to particular user action eg clicking on button
- Routines/code for handling events
- Predefined routines for the creation of buttons/windows/forms/etc

(*g*) *Any two from:*
- Comment lines/internal documentation to describe code
- Capitalise/highlight/embolden keywords to increase readability
- Indentation/blank lines/white space to increase readability
- Meaningful variable/subroutine/function names describes function of code
- Modular code/use of procedures/functions
- Use of parameter passing
- Use of local variables
- Any other valid

(*h*) (i) A variable that can be used/accessed/updated anywhere in a program.

(ii) *Any one from:*
- Unexpected changes to variables caused by variables with the same name interacting
- Data flow is unclear which reduces readability
- RAM assigned to local variables is reused, so more efficient use of memory
- Any other valid response with explanation

17. (*a*) *Any two from:*
- Interpreter will translate the contents of the loops every time they are carried out
- Compiler will translate the contents of the loops once only
- Saving processor time by reducing the number of translations

(*b*) *Any one from:*
Font, size, style, colour, columns/table/tab, alignment

(*c*) Perfective

(*d*) (i)
- Number of floors in the building
- Number of rooms on each floor

(ii)
- Passed by value
- The subprogram only needs to use these values, it should not change them

(*e*) Set min to first temp in array
Set max to first temp in array

For each temp()
    If temp(current)>max then
       Set max to temp(current)

    If temp(current)<min then
       Set min to temp(current)
    End If
Next temp()

SECTION III

Part A – Artificial Intelligence

18. (a) (i) *Any one from:*
- Machines/computers/programs capable of doing task that would require intelligence if done by human
- Ability of computer to show intelligent behaviour
- Any other valid

(ii) Turing test

(iii) *Any one from:*
- A human requires intelligence to play the game so the computer is intelligent if it can play/beat the human
- Games have a restricted rule set and a clear goal so they are easier to program
- Games are able to be expressed as logical rules so can be coded easily
- Any other valid fact with explanation

(b) (i) *Any two from:*
- Learning
- Problem solving skills
- Remember facts/experiences
- Language
- Creativity

(ii) *Any one (matching answer to part (i))from:*
- Learning new strategies that can be applied in future games
- Problem solving to search for appropriate strategy for different situations that occur
- Remembering previous experience to inform future strategy
- Interpreting of typed or spoken commands to perform actions
- The idea of coping with new situations and/or novel solutions

(c) (i) *Any one from:*
- Different processors evaluate different paths/move) simultaneously
- Several possible moves explored independently at same time

(ii) *Any one from:*
- With more states held in memory, response time should be faster
- A larger amount of game data/states can be stored improving experience and decision making
- Allowing more moves to be stored more complex games can be played
- Valid point leading to improved performance

19. (a) *Any one from:*
- Both systems take a number of inputs
- The strengths of the inputs are totalled
- Both systems use weightings (to boost or inhibit signals)
- If the total value of inputs in each system is greater than a threshold value the neuron fires

(b) • Alter weights
- Alter threshold values

(c) (i) Containing knowledge about a specialised/narrow area eg character recognition, weather forecasting

(ii) *Any one from:*
- Large known data set or large set of examples for which the output can be given
- Finite set of characteristics for inputs
- Numerical values for inputs or conversion to numerical eg female=1, male=2

(d) *Any one from:*
- Software model is more easily programmed/reprogrammed/adapted/updated hard-wired solutions must be rebuilt
- Software model is easily duplicated for testing/training/distribution each hard-wired unit must be built
- Any other valid comparison showing advantage of software model

20. (a) (i) • Image acquisition
- Capturing the (digitised) image

(ii) *Any one from:*
- Overlapping people will confuse the outlines making outlines (of individual swimmers) difficult to detect
- Shadows being cast/reflections which will create false edges
- Waves/ripples/distortions in the water will distort the outlines making false edges
- Any valid problem with explanation

(b) 16 bits or 2 bytes

21. (a) • X=atlas_bear
- X=eastern_elk

(b) earlier(A twentieth)

(c) • Match at 11, Y is instantiated to sea_cow, <u>subgoal is extinct(X, A)</u>
- Match at 1, X is instantiated to dodo and A instantiated to seventeenth, <u>second sub-goal extinct(sea_cow,B)</u>
- Match at 2, B instantiated to eighteenth, <u>subgoal earlier(seventeenth, eighteenth)</u>
- Match at 9, <u>subgoal older(seventeenth,eighteenth)</u>
- Match at 6, all subgoals met, <u>output X=dodo</u>

(d) Flips/toggles/reverses output (from true to false or vice versa)

(e) (i)

(ii) • Relationships are identified (using arrowed lines)
- Objects are represented by nodes

(f) *Any one from:*
- In-built searching/pattern matching/inference engine
- Goal directed searches using queries
- Use of recursion
- No algorithm to be programmed
- Any other acceptable

22. (a) DPXLFSTEC

(b) (i) *Any one from:*
- Uses less memory/memory efficient (as it only stores the current path)
- May find 'lucky' solution on left branch

(ii) The first solution it finds is always the optimal/best solution/shortest path

(c) (i) Depth-first

(ii) • When a node has no further descendents (X, F, S, T, etc) it is abandoned (removed from memory)
- The search goes back to the previous node evaluated to identify another possible descendant

(d) • Calculates/evaluates all the descendant nodes/possible next moves (from node D)
- Selects the most promising (using an evaluation function/score)
- Moves to that node/makes that move and repeats the process until goal is found

SECTION III

Part B – Computing Networking

23. (*a*) The domain name server will:
- Look up Domain Name/URL/Web Address in its database/file/list
- Perform domain name resolution/find its <u>IP address</u>/translate URL into <u>IP address</u>
- Return IP address to user's machine/browser or route connection for communication

(*b*) *Any one from:*
- Denial of service attack – jamming the website with bogus queries **or** bandwidth consumption/resource starvation
- Phishing – criminals setting up a clone of the site to gather card details
- Any other valid responses with description

(*c*) Class C

And any one from:
- No more than 254 addresses can be assigned (the hotel does not need this many)
- Class C would waste fewer IP addresses
- Other classes have too many IP addresses

(*d*) (i) *Any one from:*
- Websites/URLs that are not allowed to be accessed are listed in the software
- Websites containing keywords can be blocked

(ii) • Selected websites/URLs are approved and listed in the software
- Only websites on the approved list can be viewed

(*e*) *Any two from:*
- Checking Internet history
- Intercept communications/e-mail/Internet phone
- Access decryption keys/encrypted data

(*f*) Spider – travels from one link to another on the web, gathering indexing information

Meta-search – transmits/passes queries to several other search engines and their databases are searched and details summarised

(*g*) *Any two from:*
- Cannot format the title tag
- No close of head
- Closing </html> is missing its "l"

(*h*) • A <u>meta tag</u> should be included (in the head section)
- Relevant keywords added to (meta) tag
- Any other valid

(*i*) *Any one from:*
- File virus – Attaches to the code of a program. It is run when the program is executed
- Boot Sector Virus – Infects startup files/boot files of the OS and is executed at startup time
- Macro Virus – A virus is a macro attached to a document and runs when the document is opened (It often copies itself to the macro library as a step towards copying itself to other files)

24. (*a*) (i) • Node checks to see if data transfer is taking place
- If no transfer is taking place, data is transmitted
- If two nodes attempt to transmit at same time **or** if a collision is detected
- Each node waits a random amount of time before attempting to re-transmit

(ii) Time is taken to (*any one from*):
- Check if line is free
- Wait a random amount of time (before re-transmitting if there was a collision)

- Increased time/traffic due to re-transmitting data

(*b*) *Any combination from:*
- Packet switching allows the network hardware to decide on the most efficient/least congested/fastest/cheapest route to take
- Circuit switching establishes a line and uses this throughout
or
- Each packet can take a different route when the network is busy/congested
- Circuit switching establishes one line and uses this throughout, (even if it is busy)
or
- Each packet can take a different route so if data is intercepted it will not be the whole file
- With circuit switching the whole file can be intercepted

25. (*a*) (i) *Any one from:*
- Synchronises the exchange of data
- Defines how connections can be established/maintained/terminated
- Performs name resolution functions turning text names for web pages into IP addresses
- Manages log-on and password authentication

(ii) Router

(*b*) *Any one from:*
- The data transfer rate is quicker as a start and stop frame is only needed for each packet with synchronous
- whereas a start and stop bit is needed for each byte with asynchronous transmission
or
- It is much more efficient because it groups characters together into packets
- rather than sending individual bytes one at a time

(*c*) (200 * 8)/100 = 16 seconds

(*d*) (i) <u>Wireless</u> network interface card/<u>Wireless</u> NIC

(ii) *Any one from:*
- A wireless NIC sends and receive signals to and from a wireless router/access point
- Holds a MAC code/address (which identifies a computer on a network)
- Accept functions of a network interface card, for example: Packaging data into frames, Data Conversion, Buffering, Auto-sensing

(*e*) *Any two from:*
- Slower transmission rates
- More subject to interference
- Range (Distance) is restricted
- Less secure if not set up properly
- Any other valid

(*f*) *Any one from:*
- Description of resource starvation
- Description of bandwidth consumption
- Taking advantage of bugs in networking software/exploit network management flaws
- Description of attacking the routers (Note: use "ping of death" is insufficient)
- Description of domain name server (DNS) attacks
- Any other valid

(*g*) (i) *Any one from:*
- Greater communication with other people via e-mail/social networking sites
- Access to more information via Internet (not just "Access to the Internet")
- Freedom of speech via on-line forums
- Other valid response

(ii) *Any one from:*
- Broader horizons/access to different cultures enriches own culture
- Gives greater access to formal and informal education
- Lack of (face-to-face) social skills
- Greater political awareness and socio-political mobility
- Other valid implication

26. (a) *Any one from:*
- Parity check will not pick up if two bits are flipped, a cyclic redundancy check can detect this type of error
- Even parity will not pick up a break in the signal, CRC would detect a badly formed packet
- CRC uses a <u>pre-defined calculation</u> (agreed by each device), Parity may differ between two machines (and cause problems)
- Any other valid comparison

(b) *Any two from:*
- Increased transfer time
- Calculations carried out at each end of transmission
- Extra data is sent eg checksum/parity

(c) *Any two from:*
- Use of anti-virus software
- Use a firewall
- Disk monitoring for possible malfunctions/Run regular diagnostic tests
- Any other valid <u>software</u> technique

(d) (i) *Any one benefit and drawback from:*
Benefit
- Makes a full backup of the network server
- Makes a copy of the configuration, software and files of the network server
- Any other valid

Drawback
- Must be kept up to date
- Backup causes a network overhead
- Any other valid

(ii) *Any one benefit and drawback from:*
Benefit
- Copies are always up-to-date
- Recovery time is very small because you just switch to the second disc
- Any other valid

Drawback
- Does not copy network configuration or software
- Mirror disk is in same device so vulnerable to physical threat
- Any other valid

SECTION III

Part C – Multimedia Technology

27. (a) Light focused onto array of <u>CCDs</u> (charge-coupled devices)
- Analogue signal sent (from CCDs) to ADC
- (ADC) converts analogue into digital

(b) No. of frames = 12 × 24 = 288
No. of pixels = 640 × 480 = 307200
File size = No. of frames × No. of pixels × bit depth
= 288 × 307200 × 8 bits
= 707788800 bits
= 88473600 bytes
= 86400 Kilobytes
= 84.375 Megabytes

(c) (i) Define/use a CLUT (Colour Look Up Table) for the animation

(ii) *Any two from:*
- The CLUT stores the (RGB) code for the colours used
- The stored colours are a reduced palette/subset of available colours
- These colours will be the colours displayed when the animation is on screen

(d) • Stores repeated patterns of data (in a dictionary)
- And stores a code to match these repeating blocks in the file

28. (a) ADC converts the analogue data into digital

(b) *Any one from:*
- WAV
- AIF/AIFF (Audio Interchange File Format)

(c) (i) Normalisation

(ii) *Any two from:*
- Average or peak volume is determined
- Relative sound levels are increased or decreased to bring all sounds within range
- Sound uses the full dynamic range available

(d) File size = Time × Sampling frequency × Depth × Channels
= 300 × 44100 × 16 × 2 bits
= 423360000 bits
= 52920000 bytes
= 51679.6875 Kb
= 50.5 Mb

(e) *Any two from:*
- More channels allow more data to be held
- Better positioning of sound output/placing of instruments
- Other valid

(f) Notes stored using a list of attributes such as instrument, pitch, volume, duration, tempo

(g) • Can edit attributes of notes
- To sound differently on different channels/to create special effects

29. (a) *Any one from:*
- Bluetooth has a slow data transfer rate and video files are very large
- Bluetooth has a limited range so camera would have to be close to computer
- Other valid reason with explanation

(b) (i) Firewire/USB2.0/USB3.0

(ii) • Smooth display of live video requires fast data transfer
- Firewire has faster data transfer than USB 2.0
- Any other valid

(c) *Any two from:*
- Compression is done locally
- Local compression allows capturing of more/longer video
- File transfer times should be reduced due to the reduced file size
- Hardware codec is faster than a software codec
- Any other valid

30. (a) *Any two from:*
- WYSIWYG means slides/frames appear as they would in a viewer/player
- Author does not have to save authoring code and then view slides/frames in different viewers/players
- Author does not have to learn authoring code to create slides/frames
- Any other valid

(b) • Key frames are stored (one every five/ten/etc)
  • <u>Each frame</u> is compressed (using lossy compression/JPEG is used)
  • Only changes between key frames are stored. (The data that stays the same in successive frames is removed)

(c) *Any one from:*
  • Resolution is limited (to a maximum of 320×240) but would be suitable for display in a small window
  • Frame rate is limited (to 30fps) but is acceptable for smooth display (above 25fps)
  • File size is limited (to 2GB) but these clips are short
  • Any other valid

(d) (i) • Container files can hold several files of different types (as per multimedia presentation)
  • Less complex download process as a single file to download
  • Single file reduces the likelihood of missing/breaking links between component parts
  • Any other valid reason with explanation

  (ii) Software/codec is needed on the receiving computer to recreate the 'contained' files

(e) *Any two from:*
  • To allow hardware decoding of video/graphics files (using DSP)
  • More (V)RAM to buffer data (using GPU)
  • Provides additional dedicated processor
  • Any other valid

31. (a) *Any two from:*
  • Smaller file size/memory/backing storage (for simple/uncomplicated graphics)
  • Resolution independent
  • Allows editing of component objects
  • Object layers can be rearranged

(b) *Any two from:*
  • Texture
  • Depth/Z-co-ordinate
  • Direction
  • Lighting

(c) *Any one from:*
  • VRML (Virtual Reality Modelling Language/Virtual Reality Markup Language)
  • WRL

COMPUTING HIGHER 2011

SECTION I

1. 1023 **or** $2^{10} - 1$

2. *Any one from:*
  • Clock speed the number of clock cycles per second
  • MIPS the number of millions of instructions per second
  • FLOPS the number of floating point operations per second
  • Application based tests assess computer performance in doing a series of real-world tasks

3. (a) *Any one from:*
  • Buffering uses RAM Spooling uses hard disk
  • Buffering is used after data is received. Spooling is used before sending data

(b) *Any two from:*
  • data format conversion
  • voltage conversion
  • protocol conversion
  • handling of status signals

4. (a) Boot sector virus

(b) • Watching
  • Delivery

5. *Any one from:*
  • Faster processors/clock speed
  • Parallel/multi-core processors
  • Larger main memory capacity
  • Larger backing storage
  • Faster data transfer rates/bandwidth
  • Wireless technology
  • NICs built into motherboards
  • Any other valid

6. (a) *Any one from:*
  • Vector graphic with many stored objects; file size of a bitmap does not increase as objects are added
  • Vector graphic may store data on shapes hidden behind others; bitmap is single layer & does not store other data
  • File size of a vector graphic increases as number of objects increases; whereas a bitmap always stays the same size

(b) (i) 2^{24} **or** 16777216 colours
  (ii) File size will increase

7. (a) Software/problem/program specification

(b) *Any one from:*
  • Problem not fully specified at the first meeting with the client
  • Further refinement/modification/clarification of the problem may be necessary
  • Client disagreement with details given in specification

8. (a) *Any one from:*
  • To identify the data/variables used at each step of the design
  • To show what data is passed to/from/in/out of procedures
  • To supply data to subprograms
  • Identify which variables will be passed as parameters
  • Identify mechanism of parameter passing (IN, OUT, IN/OUT)
  • Other valid

(b) *Any two from:*
- Easy to understand/it uses English words
- Easy to convert into program code/line by line translation
- Structure of pseudocode reflects structure of modular code
- (Numbered) steps to show order/logic
- Indentation to emphasise command structures
- Pseudocode is not language specific
- Other valid

9. Stores value true/false, 1/0

10. (a) *Any one from:*
- Sections/subprograms are easily identified/implemented/tested/de-bugged/edited
- Sections/subprograms increase readability
- Independent subprograms can be added or removed easily
- Any other valid response

(b) *Any one from:*
- Internal Commentary
- Meaningful variable names
- Effective use of white space/indentation/blank lines
- Other valid

(c) *Any one from:*
- A function can only return a single value. A procedure can return any number of values
- The value of a function can be assigned to a variable. A procedure has no value

11. (a) Concatenation

(b) String

12. (a) Scripting language

(b) *Any two from:*
- Can create operations that are not readily available within the menus of the application/increase functionality
- A novice user can more easily perform complex actions
- Complex actions can be triggered by simple combination of key presses, making it easier to perform
- Access to low level operations (not available in menus)
- Adapt/alter user interface
- Same sequence of actions carried out each time the macro is run
- Other valid

SECTION II

13. (a) *Any two from:*
- Cache memory is more expensive (per megabyte)
- Cache memory has faster <u>access</u>
- Cache is Static RAM (SRAM) instead of Dynamic RAM (DRAM)
- Cache is on (or immediately adjacent to) the processor

(b) (i) *Any one from:*
- 16 GB = 137438953472bits
- 2^32 = 4294967296 memory locations
- (13743895347)/(4294967296) = 32 (bits or lines)

- 2^32 * d = 16 GB
- d = 137438953472bits/4294967296
- d = 32

- 2^{32} = 4 G
- 16/4 = 4 bytes
- 4 × 8 = 32 (bits or lines)

(ii) *Any one from:*
- Cost of RAM
- Most programs do not require maximum RAM to be installed
- Multiple addresses per location/byte addressable memory

- Some addresses assigned to I/O ports (memory mapped I/O)
- Other valid

(iii) Addressable memory size <u>doubles/increased to 32 Gb</u>

(c) • Address bus carries/holds/transfers memory address
- Data bus carries/holds/transfers data from memory location/to the processor
- Read line is activated/flagged

(d) (i) *Any one from:*
- Type of systems software that carries out a housekeeping/maintenance/support task
- Systems software which is not part of the main operating system
- Other valid

(ii) *Any two from:*
- Parts of file/unused blocks are spread across disk surface
- Each separate block/part of file requires a separate disk access
- Slows down the loading/writing of files/multiple disk access for single file

(e) *Any one from:*
- Checksum
- Heuristic detection
- (Use of) virus signatures
- Memory resident monitoring

14. (a) (i) • A client server network allows for centralised backup as all data stored on the server
- Peer-to-peer stored files across all machines so each machine has to be backed up

(ii) *Any one from:*
- No additional server/network operating system cost as peer-to-peer does not need a server/network OS
- Easy to extend as they only need to connect further machines to switch/hub etc
- Less technical knowledge required as they do not have to configure clients/server
- Security not an issue due to closed environment
- Other valid reason with suitable explanation

(b) (i)

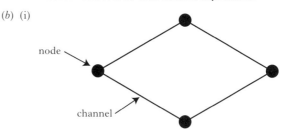

(ii) *Any one from:*
Star
- as whole network does not fail due to single channel failure
- is easier to extend by adding another branch
- any other valid
Bus
- simpler/easier to set up as it is a single wire
- easy to extend, as devices just connect to spine
- any other valid

(c) (i) *Any two from:*
- Print resolution/dpi
- Number of colours/colour depth/black & white/grey scale
- Print speed/ppm
- Buffer capacity/amount of RAM
- Type of interface/data transfer speed/serial to parallel
- Operating System/Driver

(ii) *Any one from:*
- Manage processes/Resource allocation ensures processor time and memory are allocated to the process
- Input output management sends and receives signals from the printer
- Memory management allocates memory and locates data in memory to be sent to printer
- Interpret user commands (CLI) receives user commands to print data
- File Management will locate and retrieve the file from backing storage
- Error reporting will report any problems with the printer, eg Printer out of paper etc.

(d) *Any one from:*
- Provides a queuing facility for print jobs
- May maximise efficiency of printer use by distributing jobs
- Stores (multiple) print jobs/jobs from (multiple) computers
- Organises/prioritises printing queue
- Other valid

(e) *Any two from:*
- Solid state storage is more robust than mechanical hard drive
- Capacities of solid state storage are increasing
- Decreasing price of solid state
- SSD has faster access times
- On board encryption facility
- Lower power requirements
- Any other valid

15. (a) *Any two from:*
- Code is attached to on-screen events eg buttons/Events trigger the code
- Predefined routines for the creation of buttons/form/GUIs etc
- Flow of control is determined by user actions

(b) (i) Procedural
(ii) *Any one from:*
- Use of subprograms, one for each service on offer
- Program control using sequence – to go through initial identification procedure, and selection – to carry out chosen service
- Range of data types are available

(c) Total=0
For each option() chosen that day
If option(current) = mobile top-up then
  add 1 to total
end if
next transaction

(d) *Any two from:*
- Testing is planned in advance/creation of a test plan
- which includes test data to be used and the expected results
- will be followed in a logical order
- Involves testing of subprograms/subroutines/components/modules/programs individually and together

(e) *Any one from:*
- Testing is as thorough as possible
- Covers a wide/full range of possibilities
- Data should in range, out of range and boundary data

(f) *Any one from:*
- Compiled version of code can be saved, no need for translation every time program is run
- Will not be translated each time program is run, more processor efficient

- Translator software not required, more memory efficient
- Compiled version is saved details of code are protected from theft/alteration/copying
- Any other valid point explanation of consequence

(g) Perfective
A new feature is being added that was not originally required

16. (a) (i) *Any one from:*
- Software performs as predicted on duplicated test runs
- Software will not stop due to design flaws
- Output is correct for all specified inputs
(ii) *Any one from:*
- No unnecessary code is included in the program, processor not required to carry out unnecessary commands
- Minimise the number of disk accesses/peripherals, reducing time processor will have to stand idle
- Simple user interface as complex interfaces take some time to draw etc
- Use of Nested IFs/Case statements to logically structure code to avoid testing unnecessary conditions
- Valid programming example explanation of processor efficiency

(b) (i) *Any one from:*
- Current value (of variable) passed into a subprogram for use
- To allow data to be passed by value
- Protect (original value of) variable from change by subprogram
(ii) *Any one from:*
- Data/variables (created within procedure and only) passed out of a subprogram
- Brand new variable is passed out of subprogram

(c) *Any one from:*
- Programmers will each be writing individual subprograms for the software required, reducing implementation time **or** so they must collaborate via meetings/project manager/detailed plan
- Will discuss how to implement the design/get help from more experienced programmer/discuss testing to reduce time wasted/find and solve problems earlier/ensure testing is systematic and comprehensive
- Any other valid technique/topic and description

(d) *Any one from:*
- Can carry out a complex operation that they could not write themselves
- Do not have to design the solution to the subproblem

(e) (i) *Any two from:*
- a list of data/(fixed) number of items
- items are the same data type/array has a single data type
- position of data identified by its position/index/element/subscript
(ii) *Any one from:*
- Parameter passing list will use one array rather than a list of variables
- Do not need to write a line of code to manipulate each data item individually, operation can be performed on each item in the array using a loop

(f) *Any one from:*
Pascal: =word[5]+word[6]+word[7] **or**
  =concat(word[5],word[6],word[7])
Java: =word.substring(4,7)
Visual Basic: = right(word,3) **or** =mid(word,5,3)
TrueBasic: = word$(5:7)

SECTION III

Part A – Artificial Intelligence

17. (*a*) (i) *Any one from:*
Problem solving, memory, learning, creativity, cognitive ability, other valid

(ii) *Any one from:*
- Uses natural language which is a high order skill
- Uses a greater variety of human intelligence skills rather than manipulate a closed world of chess rules
- Requires the integration of human intelligence (in the same way that people do) instead of following of best path
- Uses judgement to decide levels of confidence for response
- Larger domain of knowledge required in quiz game, Chess has a much narrower simplistic domain
- Any other valid with justification in context

(*b*) (i) *Any two from:*
- Natural Language Understanding NLU – checking it is a valid sentence, extracting meaning for the sentence/phrase, resolve ambiguity
- Natural Language Generation NLG – formulating a suitable response to the sentence/question
- Speech Synthesis – outputting the response in the form of sound/voice

(ii) *Any one from:*
- "ship of the desert" is a metaphor/ambiguous which could prove difficult because its literal sense is impossible
- question/answer on 'surfing' is an example of changing nature of language, ambiguity used within the question/answer

(*c*) *Any one from:*
Faster processors would execute searches of knowledge in less time.
Parallel processing:
- would enable multiple responses to be evaluated simultaneously
- to search possible responses to select the one to use

Cache
- would shorten the time for fetching and executing instructions to arrive at a response more quickly.

18. (*a*) (i) *Any one from:*
Inference engine – performs pattern matching/searching on the rules using information gathered
User interface – gathers information from the user by presenting options/choices and provides output to user

(ii) *Any one from:*
- Asking the user questions (to add responses)
- By selecting/applying rules (and adding the conclusion)

(*b*) (i) *Any one from:*
Determines if the software is fit for purpose by meeting the software specification
Determines if the software is correct by giving the correct output for the specified input
Determines if the software is robust by handling invalid input

(ii) *Any one from:*
- Only the lawyers have the knowledge to know if the output is correct
- Only the lawyers will understand the terminology of the output documents
- Any other reasonable response

(*c*) Internet makes it available to users worldwide but laws vary from country to country or region to region

(*d*) *Any one from:*
Laws can change requiring maintenance
Novel situations for which there are no applicable rules
No common sense so limited to application of existing facts/rules
Expert system may be out of date Lawyer has more up-to-date knowledge
Any other reasonable situation with description

(*e*) *Any one from:*

Dendral	identifying unknown organic molecules
Mycin	identify bacteria causing severe infections
Rice-Crop Doctor	diagnoses pests and diseases for rice crops
AGREX/CALEX	areas of fertilizer application, crop protection, irrigation scheduling, and diagnosis of diseases
Variex	advises selection of the best cultivators for different agricultural situations
Weiping Jin Expert System	advice on crop management
LEY Expert System	automated, remote, real-time weather data acquisition and reporting system
CLIPS	to reach conclusions concerning profitable alfalfa production
CaDet	decision support system for Early Cancer Detection
DXplain	Medical diagnosis
Puff	diagnoses the results of pulmonary function tests
Seth	advice concerning the treatment and monitoring of drug poisoning
PEIRS	(Pathology Expert Interpretative Reporting System) appends interpretative comments to chemical pathology reports
R1 or XCON or XSEL	automatically selecting the computer system components based on the customer's requirements.

19. (*a*) (i) ●●●○_○○ or bbbw_ww

(ii) *Any one from:*
●_●●○○○ or b_bbwww
●●○●_○○ or bbwb_ww

(iii) *Any two from:*
- A path ends, or is blocked, as there are no possible other moves/descendants – there are no more legal moves for the stones from this point
- The algorithm moves back to the previously stored state/move/arrangement of stones
- To evaluate another possible move/descendant – try to move a different stone

(*b*) • The first solution it finds is always the best solution.
• Won't get stuck in a loop down one branch.

(*c*) Heuristic (search)

20. (*a*)

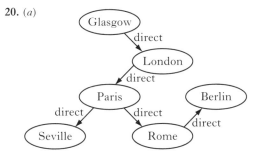

(*b*) Part of a rule that is satisfied for the goal to be satisfied/met

(*c*) X=rome, X=seville

(*d*) ?direct(X, rome), direct(X, seville)
?fly_direct(X rome) AND fly_direct(X seville)

(*e*) • Match at 7 X instantiated to glasgow, sub_goal
  <u>fly_direct(glasgow, Z)</u>
• Match at 6 P instantiated to glasgow, sub_goal
  <u>direct(glasgow, Q)</u>
• Match at 1 <u>Q instantiated to london</u>   **or**
  <u>Z instantiated to london</u>
• Second sub-goal of rule 7, <u>fly_direct(london, Y)</u>
• Match at 6 P instantiated to london, sub_goal
  <u>direct(london, Q)</u>
• Match at 2 Q instantiated to paris/Y instantiated to paris.
  <u>Y=paris is output</u>

SECTION III

Part B – Computer Networking

21. (*a*) A – html
  B – title
  C – body

(*b*) Project Manager

(*c*) (i) *Any one from:*
  • Can check availability of activities instantly so if not available, you can easily check another one
  • Less chance of "worker"/"human" error as you can check the final screen
  • Pay before going on holiday so you don't need as much money with you on holiday/reduces queuing when on holiday
  • Know in advance what activities you will be taking part in so can bring requirements with you (for example: swimming suit)
  • Can book 24/7 so are not confined to normal office hours/more chance to make booking
  • Can book from any location so no need to travel to location/take time out of holiday to make booking
  • Any other valid benefit with appropriate reasoning

(ii) *Any one from:*
  • Customers may not think of the cost as "holiday money"
  • Some activities "look better" online
  • Good advertising
  • Customers have more time to book (24/7)
  • Any other valid answer

(iii) *Any one from:*
  • Use a secure protocol such as HTTPS
  • Encryption
  • Digital certificates
  • Use a secure 3rd party payment service
  • Any other valid answer

(*d*) • WML doesn't support many text formats
  • WML has problems with tables (due to their width)
  • Restricted graphic format/standard JPG/GIF/PNG Web formats cannot be displayed without conversion (to WBMP format)
  • Any other valid answer

22. (*a*) 200 * 8 * 1024 = 1,638,400 Kilobits
  1,638,400 Kilobits/512/60 = 53.3 minutes

(*b*) *Any two from*
  • To standardise the transmission of data between computer systems on networks
  • To allow different computer systems to communicate and work together on a network
  • To show how different protocols work at different levels in a network OS/environment

(*c*) (i) • IP adds an address (header) to each packet
    • IP routes the packets around the network
  (ii) File Transfer Protocol/FTP

(*d*) *Any one from:*
  • The message is divided into packets
  • Each individual packet can take a different path through the network
  • Packets are re-assembled at destination

(*e*) (i) • Double errors cancel each other out so error would not be spotted
    • For example: when using even parity, 0001 001 with parity bit 0 is received as 1000 001 with parity bit 0, the parity check will not fail since the reversal of the 1st and 4th bits leaves the parity bit unchanged
  or
    • Where sender and receiver are using different parities
    • For example: when using even parity; 0001 001 with parity bit 0 is received as 0000 001 with parity bit 0 which should indicate an error, but the receiver is using odd parity and therefore parity check would not fail

  (ii) *Any one from:*
    • (Time will be taken to) carry out the calculation of the parity bit
    • (Time will be taken to) send the extra parity bit
    • (Time will be taken to) perform the parity check

23. (*a*) (i) Denial of Service Attack/DOS
  (ii) *Any two from:*
    • Loss of business
    • Cost of employing experts to analyse the attack
    • Cost of placing preventative measures for future attacks
  (iii) *Any two from:*
    • IP address filtering/Filters out IP addresses/block selected IP addresses access to local area network
    • Prevents access to network from particular ports/monitor all communication ports
    • Inspects incoming packets for suspicious activity

(*b*) • *Any two from:*
  • A switch reduces network traffic due to it directing the packet/data to a specific station
  • There are fewer collisions due to a switch allocating the whole bandwidth to each connected computer

(*c*) (i) • The first octet is between <u>192</u> and <u>223</u>
    • The first three octets are fixed
  (ii) It is different to the original which <u>indicates a different network</u>
  (iii) It is <u>greater than 255/Out of range</u>

(d) *Any two from:*
  - If more than one transmission takes place there will be a collision and data will have to <u>wait a random amount of time</u>
  - If more than one transmission takes place there will be a collision and data will have to be <u>re-sent</u>
  - Before transmitting data time is taken to check if the line is free

24. (a) (i) • A meta-search engine transmits/passes queries to several other search engines
      - and their databases are searched
      - and details summarised in a list
  (ii) Spiders **or** Meta-Tags

  (b) SMTP is used for <u>sending/transfer/transmit</u> e-mails

  (c) *Any two from:*
    - Lack of face to face communication/social skills
    - Health issues/lack of exercise
    - Safety issues/access to inappropriate people
    - Security issues/children giving out personal details
    - Access to inappropriate material
    - Any other appropriate answer

  (d) (i) There is a list of acceptable websites
      - restricted view of the Internet
      - all other websites are blocked
    (ii) *Any one from:*
      - Number of web sites that could be viewed is too limited.
      - Child can only access websites deemed suitable by the parent.
    (iii) This filters out particular keywords/websites and allows access to all others.

  (e) (i) Access to a broad range of information **and** the skill to use it.
    (ii) *Any two from:*
      Information Rich enables you to:
      - Make informed decisions and choices
      - Inform individual and business research/projects/tasks
      - Facilitate individual educational progress
      - Improve individual leisure pursuits
      - Improve individual job prospects
      - Any other valid answer

SECTION III

Part C – Multimedia Technology

25. (a) (i) • Scanner uses single linear CCD(s)
      - Digital camera uses a CCD array/grid
    (ii) Uses intermediate shades of colour in surrounding pixels
    (iii) Rescan the logo using a higher resolution than the original scan.
      or
      Software adds extra <u>smaller</u> pixels to blend in.

  (b) *Any one from:*
    - Vector graphic is resolution independent and so will always be displayed to the best effect
    - Logo is few objects and so vector graphic will have a small file size

26. (a) (i) Data being transferred and viewed before entire file has been received
    (ii) • No permanent copy of file stored on visitor's computer
      - So reduces opportunity for illegal copying

(b) • To decompress the streamed file
  - To decrease transfer time

(c) *Any two from:*
  - Hardware codecs use own GPU/processor rather than CPU
  - Coding/decoding will consequently be quicker
  - and so file can be played at correct rate

(d) *Any one from:*
  Volume/Instrument/Pitch/Channel

(e) Voice or other recorded/sampled sound

(f) (i) • MIDI files are easy to manipulate
      - Individual attributes can be changed
  (ii) *Any one from:*
    - Sound card generates sound from MIDI file depends on capability of sound card/may not be same as original recording.
    - MP3 is a bit mapped/sampled sound so the original sound is not reproduced.
    - Valid fact with valid explanation
  (iii) • MP3 does not store sounds that humans cannot hear/emphasises sounds humans can hear best
    - MP3 does not store sounds that are drowned out by louder sounds
    - and then uses the Huffman compression technique.

27. (a) (i) • Can plan the order of the clips/the effects to be applied.
    (ii) *Any one from:*
      Fade/Wipe/Dissolve/Hard cut/Peel/page turn/any other valid

  (b) File size = $(4 \times 60 \times 15) = 3600$ frames
        = **3600** $\times (24 \times 720000)$ bits
        = 62208000000 bits = 7776000000 bytes = 7.24 Gb

  (c) • Key frames are stored (one every five/ten/etc)
    - Each frame is compressed (using lossy compression/JPEG is used)
    - Only changes between key frames are stored. (The data that stays the same in successive frames is removed)

  (d) *Any one from:*
    - Frame size/resolution is limited (to a maximum of 320 by 240) but would be suitable for display in a small window
    - Frame rate is limited (to 30fps) but is acceptable for smooth display (above 25fps)

  (e) • ADC converts analogue data into digital data
    - DSP compresses/adds effects to digital data

28. (a) File size = $(60 \times 44100) \times 2 \times 32$ bits
        = 169344000 bits = 20.2 Mb

  (b) PCM (Pulse Code Modulation)

  (c) (i) A container file allows the storage of a variety of data types as a single file.
    (ii) *Any two from:*
      All necessary files can be distributed as single item more likely that customer will receive all that is required for lesson.
      RIFF is a common file format and accessible by different platforms.

  (d) (i) Normalisation
      Any one from:
      - Increases or decreases the sound levels to an average value.
      - Causes sound levels to use the full dynamic range available.

(ii) Clipping

(iii) *Any one from:*
- Volume edited to beyond the dynamic range
- A special effect may have been added.

(e) (i) • DVDs have data on 1 or 2 sides of the disc
- Holographic discs have the data stored through the thickness of the disc/in more than 2 layers

(ii) • Holographic discs can be read in parallel
- Whereas DVDs are read one layer at a time

COMPUTING HIGHER 2012

SECTION I

1. 585

2. (a) Exponent

(b) Mantissa

3. *Any two from:*
- Each pixel represented as a binary number
- As a (2D) <u>array/grid</u> of pixels
- Colour (of pixel) represented by (unique) binary value/notion of bit depth

4. *Any two from:*
- Voltage conversion
- Data format conversion/serial to parallel/analogue to digital
- Handling of status signals (accept a valid example)

5. • 1) Registers
- 3) RAM/ROM/Main Memory

6. (a) *Any two from:*
- Decide where on backing store the file will be saved
- Allocate/record address of file
- Ensure that file does not overwrite existing/valid data
- Define access rights
- Record the creation date
- Update the file directory
- Any other valid

(b) *Any one from:*
- Copies/transfers the blocks of <u>data</u> from main memory to the hard disk
- Handles errors during data transfer
- Inputting user commands for save via mouse click etc.
- Any other valid

7. (a) Bus

(b) *Any one from:*
- Better security/control of access
- Efficient backup of centralised files
- File/application sharing is simpler to set up
- Any other valid

(c) *Any one from:*
- A router
- A (cable) modem
- Any other valid

8. • The process may revisit an earlier stage
- In the light of experience/information gained

9. A problem is broken down into smaller/easier to solve (sub-)problems.

10. *Any one from:*
- Structure chart/diagram
- Flowchart
- Semantic net
- Any other valid

11. (a) *Any one from:*
- Implementation
- Testing
- Maintenance

(b) Implementation: lines of code are translated and executed in turn, reporting syntax errors
Testing: test all (or part) of code to help identify line where error occurs
Maintenance: as above

12. *Any one from:*
    - Scripting language is embedded within an application whereas a procedural is stand-alone
    - Keywords within a scripting language are specific to parent application whereas in a procedural keywords are more general
    - Programmer has control over data types/might have access to low level commands/operations in a procedural language whereas data types are embedded in a scripting language

13. (*a*) A variable which can have only 2 values – true/false

    (*b*) *Any one from:*
    - Used to terminate the loop
    - Used to show the presence of the item in the list

14. Reliable software:
    Any one from:
    - Will give correct output to valid data
    - Will not stop due to design flaws/errors
    - Free from design and coding bugs
    Robust software will not crash when invalid data is entered

15. *Any one from:*
    - Will detail test data originally used so that re-testing on that data will not need to be done again
    - Details the original test data which did not find the error
    - Allows identification of new data sets that should be tested

16. *Any two from:*
    - Use of meaningful variable names
    - Use of internal comments
    - Effective use of white space
    - Use of procedures/modularity/subroutines/functions
    - Use of parameter passing/local variables
    - Use of module libraries
    - Use of formatted keywords
    - Any other valid

SECTION II

17. (*a*) *Any one from:*
    - Clock speed does not take other important architectural features into consideration (such as data bus width)
    - Clock speed is not a measure of actual throughput.
    - Clock speed is only valid if the processors being compared have the same architecture.

    (*b*) *Any two from:*
    - FLOPS result may be more reliable as (logic/arithmetic) operations independent of level of complexity
    - Complexity of instructions used can vary (and therefore skew the results with MIPS)
    - MIPS test may have been performed with small/simple machine instructions

    (*c*) Addressable memory = 2^{32} x 128
    = 549755813888 bits =68719476736 bytes
    = 67108864 Kbytes = 65536 Mbytes = 64Gbytes.

    (*d*) (i) AND, OR, NOT, =, <, <=, >, >=, <>, etc.

    (ii) *Any one from:*
    - Synchronise processor instructions/operations
    - Control the flow of data/instructions within CPU
    - Activate and/or respond to control lines
    - Control fetch execute cycle
    - Decode and execute instructions.

    (*e*) More data can be carried in a single instruction cycle/at one time

18. (*a*) *Any two from:*
    - Each computer on a network has its own built in processor/RAM/backing storage
    - A terminal is reliant on the processor/RAM/backing storage capacity of the mainframe
    - A mainframe will have many thousands of processors / massive ram space/ backing storage
    - Much more than any individual computer on a computer network

    (*b*) (i) • The available free space is fragmented, file fragments/space spread out over the disks
    - Large section of (contiguous) free space required to store the file
    or
    - Disk contains unidentified bad sectors
    - These are unavailable for storing of data
    or
    - Disk space used by copies of virus that does not show in file table
    - But these blocks are unavailable for storing data

    (ii) A defragmenter
    or
    disk editor
    or
    anti-virus

    (iii) Utility software

    (*c*) Copper/UTP/fibre optic/co-axial/wireless/WiFi
    Any valid reason (range/bandwidth/security) that allows at least 80 metres range with large files

    (*d*) Address (of the data to be read) placed on the address bus (by the processor)
    The read line is set high/activated
    Data (from the memory location) transferred (to the processor) using the data bus

19. (*a*) Unicode
    Unicode can represent all 3000 chars, ASCII can only represent up to 256/8 bit

    (*b*) *Any two from:*
    - DPI/Resolution
    - Compatibility/interface
    - Buffer capacity
    - Printing speed/PPM
    - Physical size/portable

    (*c*) (i) A file virus cannot infect a data file only an executable file

    (ii) A virus is (self-)<u>replicating</u> code

    (iii) *Any one from:*
    - Camouflage
    - Watching
    - Delivery
    - Replication

    (*d*) *Any two from:*
    - <u>8 bit colour/8 bits per pixel</u>/256 colours
    - Bitmapped format
    - Transparency
    - (Lossless) compression {but not lossy compression}
    - Supports simple animation
    - Standard file format (high level of compatibility)

SECTION II SDP

20. (a) (i) *Any one from:*
- (Interview client management) to establish <u>precisely</u> what is needed elicit details
- (Interview current users of the system) to establish good/bad points of current system
- Any other valid explanation

(ii) *Any two from:*
- Issue questionnaires
- Make observation notes/observe current practice
- Examine sources of information/company documentation

(b) (i) Software specification/program specification/ORD

(ii) *Any two from:*
- Formalises the <u>details</u> of the software to be produced
- It will form part of a legal agreement/contract
- If one of client s needs is omitted from the document, it will not be done as part of the initial contract
- Additional features cannot be added into software without new contract
- Any other valid reason

(c) *Any one from:*
- Contribute to the provision of test data
- Plan structure of testing to match boundaries/analysis
- Validate test data to be used at testing stage
- Validate test results against specification
- Any other valid

(d) Since he has involvement with the project he doesn t qualify

(e) Systematic
- Tests individual subroutines, then modules, up to whole system testing
- Methodical/logical/planned checking of software

Comprehensive
- Uses normal/extreme/exceptional data
- Test software in as many cases as possible/full range

(f) Project manager

21. (a) (1-D) Array of real

(b)
```
tallest = height[1]
name_of_winner = name[1]
loop to end of list
    if height[position]>tallest then
        tallest = height[position]
        name_of_winner = name[position]
    end if
end loop
display name_of_winner (1 mark)
```
or
```
max = 1
for position = 1 to end of list  do
    if height[position]> height[max] then
        max = position
    end if
end loop
display name[max]
```

(c) (i) *Any one from:*
- Change initial condition to smallest = height[1]
- Change > to < OR 'change greater than to less than'
- Change variable names to eg tallest to smallest / max to min
- Change output line

(ii) *Any one from:*
- Change initial condition to smallest = height[1] which can be reset when a lower value is found
- Change > to < since looking for smaller values than the current one
- Change variable names to eg tallest to smallest/max to min to reflect meaningful variable names
- Change output line to reflect change in variable name/new context if name is in descriptive text

22. (a) The first IF is true, but the second and third IFs will still be evaluated wasting processor time

(b) <u>Nested IF</u>
```
IF cost per person is less than 500
    set band to 'cheap'
ELSE IF (cost per person less than 2000)
    set band to 'medium';
ELSE
    Set band to 'expensive';
(END IF)
```
or ... <u>CASE statement</u>
```
CASE cost per person OF
    IS < 500 : set band to 'cheap';
    IS < 2000 : set band to 'medium';
Otherwise
    Set band to 'expensive'
(END CASE)
```

(c) By value since the value is not being changed in the procedure

(d) Joining/adding together of (sub-)strings

(e) A (self-contained/discrete/named) module/unit/block/section of code which has a value/returns a single value to the calling program

SECTION III PART A: ARTIFICIAL INTELLIGENCE

23. (a) Test a system/device/program for presence of (artificial) intelligence

(b) *Any two from:*
- Identifies keywords/phrases from human sentence
- Matches an appropriate response (from bank)
- If there isn t a match, makes a generic response or another start point

(c) *Any two from:*
- May fail to store previous responses
- Inability to include current or topical statements
- Inability to problem solve in conversation
- Inability to comprehend humour/emotion
- Vocabulary/grammar may be artificial/unusual
- Any other valid

(d) Any one of increased clock speed/presence of cache/increased cache/multiple processors

Any valid description of how performance is improved ie
- Multiple threads/queries improving searching/pattern matching
- Faster execution producing faster responses

24. (a) Problem solving

(b) The computer is merely following instructions of the (intelligent) programmer/human.

(c) Search tree

(d) Breadth-first (1) because
- All possible descendants from the start state have been generated
- Node(0,5) would not be generated yet in depth-first
- Node(3,5) would have been discarded in depth-first

(e) Depth-first and Heuristic

(f) (0,3)

(g) *Any two from:*
- Empty 3 litre jug
- Empty 5 litre jug
- Fill the 3 litre jug from the 5 litre jug/Pour the 5 litre jug into the 3 litre jug

25. (a) *Any two from:*
- Flat/ two-dimensional viewpoint, eliminating/reducing problems with 3D depth perception
- Light variation/shadows have been reduced/eliminated by the use of a lamp
- Edge detection of rectangular objects with straight lines is simpler.
- Tiles on known background colour/conveyor belt

(b) 32 bit colour= 4294967296 (accept 2^{32})

(c) *Any two from:*
- Signal processing convert signal into form that can be understood/ digitisation /"clean up" signal
- Edge detection identify sharp changes in colour/tone/ light as edges, making a wireframe model
- Object recognition wireframe model is matched against templates of known objects
- Image understanding analysis of collection of objects give sense of whole image

(d) *Any three from:*
- Weights will be initially set
- Known inputs will be used and outputs compared to expected
- Weights altered/rebalanced to achieve the known output
- Process repeated until all inputs and outputs match

(e) *Any one from:*
- Vision system for lane control in a car.
- Vision system used to inform sat nav
- Any other valid vision system <u>embedded</u> in a larger system

26. (a) *Any one from:*
- Machines/computers/programs capable of doing task that would require intelligence if done by human
- Ability of system to display/emulate intelligent human behaviour
- Any other valid

(b) *Any one from:*
- Ability to make decisions independent of external control
- The ability to learn/problem solve/etc
- Any other valid

(c) *Any two from:*
- Power supply - battery needs recharging, attaching power cable hinders mobility
- Vision system - detecting and avoiding obstacles/stairs
- Navigation - planning a path or limiting the path using virtual walls across doorways
- Type of terrain - choosing tools for cleaning different surfaces

Note: the marks could come from the same bullet

(d) (i) Where responsibility lies in the event of an accident (or other valid)

(ii) *Any one from:*
- Use a disclaimer (denying responsibility for accidents caused by not following instructions.)
- Any method of avoiding accidents such as audible signals etc.
- Any other valid

27. (a) X=druid

(b) ? is_weapon_against(X troll)

(c) • life_points(troll, 800) would be false/no.
- not(life_points(troll, 800)) would be true

(d) • Match at 13 X instantiated to troll, <u>subgoal has_found(troll Z)</u>
- Match at 1 Z instantiated to jewel, <u>subgoal is_weapon_against(jewel Y)</u>
- Match at 8, Y=troll, new <u>subgoal troll=troll is true</u>
- <u>not(troll=troll) is false,</u> subgoal fails
- Backtrack to match at 2, Z instantiated to sword, new subgoal <u>is_weapon_against(sword, Y)</u>
- Match at 7, Y=orc <u>not(troll=orc) succeeds</u>
- <u>Output Y=orc</u>

(e) (i) stronger_than(X Y)

(ii) Corrective

SECTION III PART B: COMPUTER NETWORKING

28. (a) (i) Network

(ii) Presentation

(b) • IP adds its own header/address header/source/ destination/IP header to each packet.
- IP routes the packets around the network.

(c) • It reduces the number of collisions on a network therefore reducing the amount of data that would have to be re-transmitted
or
- It reduces simultaneous transmissions therefore reducing collisions

(d) Odd Parity
Any one justification from:
- there is an odd number of ones/zeros
- five ones to be transmitted
- there was an even number of ones before the parity bit was added

(e) Asynchronous
Any one from:
- Asynchronous uses start and stop bits around each byte/character/word
- Synchronous uses a start and stop **frame** for each **packet** of data. It does **not** use a start/stop bit.

29. (a) *Any one from:*
- Security - computers must be physically connected to access the network/<u>harder</u> to intercept data
- <u>Less</u> interference/signal drop-off
- Bandwidth - Faster transmission speeds

(b) Passive Attack

(c) <title> White Tooth </title>

(d) *Any one from:*
- 16,777,216 colours
- 16.7 million colour
- 2^{24} colours
- 24 bit colour

(e) (i) Metatag (with keywords)

(ii) Header/head

(f) (i) Wireless Markup Language/WML

(ii) WAP

(iii) PDA/palmtop/Pager/2-way Radio/Any other valid

(g) Corrective

30. (a) Telnet

(b) (i) *Any one from:*
- Bandwidth consumption - This degrades the server performance by sending a large number of data packets in a short period of time.
- Resource starvation - An attack which is intended to use resources that would bring the network down. For example, an e-mail inbox could be bombarded with e-mails and so would fill up and therefore not allow genuine e-mails through.
- Programming flaws - This takes advantage of bugs in networking software.
- Attacking the routers - This involves "hi-jacking" data packets and routing them to the target server, which then gets flooded with data packets, or re-directing them to false addresses.
- Domain Name Server attacks/IP Spoofing - This involves sending a large number of DNS queries with a spoofed IP address of the target server. The DNS then floods the target server with an excessive amount of replies.

(ii) *Any two from:*
- Cost of determining the nature of the attack
- Cost of repair and response to the attack
- Cost of devising and implementing safeguards
- Cost of additional admin to compensate for loss of network services
- Any other valid cost

(c) *Any two from:*
- Monitors all communication ports/checks packets/block ports
- Keeps track of all communications/makes user log
- Blocks unauthorised access/prevents unsolicited traffic
- IP Filtering

(d) *Any two from:*
- Authenticate the user − a "callback" facility to correct phone line/IP address
- Set user permissions allocating the minimum necessary access to each user/levels of access
- Encrypting data to make data unreadable/give each employee a restricted key
- Use a secure protocol such as HTTPS to make data unreadable in transit
- Other valid method showing how it prevents access

(e) *Any two from:*
- It creates a backup
- Which allows data to be saved to several disks at the same time
- Creates an exact /up-to-date copy of the data on the server

(f) (i) • List of approved website/URLs (in the software)
- Only approved websites can be viewed/all others are blocked

(ii) *Any one from:*
- Unsuitable websites/URLs are listed in the Internet Filtering software
- Websites containing certain keywords/content/file types/domain names can be blocked

(g) *Any one from:*
- Uses wireless transmission/no cables
- Across a very short range
- Low power consumption
- Any other valid

31. (a) *Any one from:*
- Class A allows 16,777,214 addresses (2^{24}- 2)
- A small network would use class C (with 254 addresses)
- Only 12 IP addresses are needed

(b) (Uniquely) identifies a computer/device (on a network).

(c) *Any three from:*
- The original/same calculation is carried out
- A comparison is made to the original
- If there is a difference, there has been an error/data will need to be retransmitted
- If the results match the data will be accepted

(d) (i) • (Splits the data into small parts and) each packet may take a different route to its destination
- Unlikely to intercept all packets/the whole file

(ii) Circuit switching

(e) (i) • (150 * 8) = 1,200 Megabits
- 1,200 / 8 = 150 seconds (/ 60 = 2.5 minutes)
  or
- 8 megabits per second = 1 megabyte per second
- 150 megabytes takes 150 seconds (/ 60 = 2.5 minutes)

(ii) *Any two from:*
- Bad packets needing re-sent/collisions of data
- Rest of message frame (parity etc) takes up space and hence bandwidth
- Another part of the network may have a slower connection
- Sharing bandwidth with other users/processes
- Integrity checks on file
- Any other valid

SECTION III PART C: MULTIMEDIA TECHNOLOGY

32. (a) (i) *Any two from:*
- Can be replayed on any musical instrument with a MIDI interface (eg keyboard, synthesiser, drum machine)
- Accuracy of playback sound not necessary for practise
- Individual instruments/notes can be edited or have effects added
- Backing tracks unlikely to include voice
- No interference/white noise/background sounds

(ii) Duration – length (number of beats) of a <u>note</u>
Tempo – speed at which music is to be replayed/ number of beats per minute (bpm)

(b) *Any two from:*
- MP3 can be played on a wider variety of players than MIDI
- MP3 produces a more natural sound
- MIDI sound can vary as same "instrument" may differ between devices
- Any other valid

(c) No. of frames = 64 × 25 = 1600
No. of pixels = 1024 × 768 = 786432

File size = No. of frames × No. of pixels x bit depth
= <u>1600 x 786432</u> × <u>24 bits</u>
= 30198988800 bits = 3774873600 bytes = 3686400 Kb
= 3600 Mb

(d) No permanent copy on pupil computer

(e) • If data buffered is viewed before next block is stored/received
- Then video is paused until next block is stored/received

33. (*a*) *Any two from:*
- Faster data transfer rate (up to 4.8 Gbits per sec)
- USB interface more common on current computer hardware
- USB3.0 has backward compatibility with previous USB interfaces
- Any other valid

(*b*) *Any one from:*
- Wireless connectivity already available (even if limited)
- WiFi reduces battery life
- Extra weight/ larger device
- Any other valid

(*c*) No moving parts/motor so less power is required

(*d*) Advantage: faster compression/processing rate
Disadvantage: cannot be (easily) upgraded

(*e*) (i) Allows an effect to be used when clips are joined together

(ii) *Any one from:*
- Wipe – line moves across first clip replacing it with next clip
- Fade out/in – clip gradually dwindles to black/ emerges from black
- Dissolve – first clip gradually morphs into next clip
- Hard cut – first clip changes instantly to next clip
- Page turn – first clip peels away from screen to show next clip
- Other valid answer – with description

(*f*) EasyVid3 and EasyVid4 data is already captured/stored in digital

34. (*a*) *Any two from:*
- Shows timing/transitions between screens
- Gives content of screens eg placement of items/layout, actual content, backgrounds, colour schemes
- Gives navigation links/hyperlinks
- Any other valid

(*b*) File size = $11000 \times 24 \times 8 \times 2$ bits
= 4224000 bits = 528000 bytes = 515.625 Kb
= 515.6 Kb

(*c*) (i) ADPCM (Adaptive Delta Pulse Code Modulation/ Adaptive Differential Pulse Code Modulation)

(ii) • Stores a sampled sound then change between sound samples (not the actual samples)
• Compression is because number of bits required to store change between samples is less than sample amplitude value.

(*d*) Storing recordings in mono would half storage required
or
Edit out pauses et cetera to shorten the clip

(*e*) Fade in

(*f*) (i) Graph must show flat (clipped) section(s)
Clipping occurs when sound outwith the dynamic range is lost

(ii) • It calculates average volume/level
• Scales amplitudes/volumes to bring everything within dynamic range

(iii) • Every sound in the file is affected therefore background noise will also be boosted

35. (*a*) • Vector graphic formats store each object (and its attributes) separately
• Adding another object requires more data to be stored (so file size increases)

(*b*) *Any two from:*
- Vector graphic formats are displayed at hardware's resolution/resolution independent
- So scaling will not affect image quality in vector
- Bitmaps become pixelated if graphic is scaled up

(*c*) It will be a lighter /paler shade of green

(*d*) (i) *Any one from:*
- Dithering uses patterns of existing colours to create illusion of additional colours (not in palette/at bit depth)
- Two (or more) adjacent coloured pixels create the illusion of another colour (not in the palette)

(ii) • PNG allows 2^{24} (16 million) colours
• More colours are not required/this is true colour

(*e*) (i) To smooth jagged edges of curves/diagonals

(ii) *Any one from:*
- Image scanned/drawn/displayed at low resolution
- Improve the look of a (low resolution/pixelated) image
- Description of other valid situation

Published by Bright Red Publishing Ltd, 6 Stafford Street, Edinburgh, EH3 7AU
Tel: 0131 220 5804, Fax: 0131 220 6710, enquiries: sales@brightredpublishing.co.uk,
www.brightredpublishing.co.uk

Official SQA answers to 978-1-84948-285-1
2008-2012